U0941401

YOUTH AND DREAM

Struggle as a Belief

Wen Zeping

Dedicated to the celebration of the 70th anniversary of the founding of the People's Rcpublic of China and the 100th anniversary of the May 4th Movement.

Contents

Note

Young people are the most energetic and have the richest dreams! The great rejuvenation of the Chinese nation will eventually become a reality in the relay struggle of the vast majority of young people!

——Xi Jinping

(Excerpt from *Speech by Xi Jinping at the 100th Anniversary of the May 4th Movement*)

New Era & Youthful Mission (Foreword I)

Thanks to this great epoch, realizing the Dream of the great rejuvenation of the Chinese nation and building a community with a shared future for mankind lead us to a new future.

With the world multi-polarization, economic globalization, cultural diversity and social informatization, how can we cope with the common challenges and move towards a better future?

While in a new era, we should shoulder our own great mission! However serious the future challenges will be, we are full of hope.

(I)

2019 is the 100th anniversary of the May 4th Movement and the 70th anniversary of the founding of the People's Republic of China. In this extraordinary year, guests from 47 Asian countries of five continents gathered in China, concerted working on building a community with a shared future for mankind.

"In the 100 years since the May 4th Movement, one generation after another of the Chinese youth have been constantly struggling for and persisting in the creation of a youthful China and a youthful Chinese nation." General Secretary Xi Jinping, while making his important speech in the commemoration of the 100th Anniversary of the

May 4th Movement, pointed out that youth is the most active and energetic force in the whole society. In them lie the hope of the country and the future of the nation. The young people of the new era are in the best period of the development of the Chinese nation and face once-in-a-blue-time opportunities for doing meritorious deeds for the people, together with the "due mission bestowed by Heaven". In the new era, they should carry on with the spirit of the May 4th Movement, shoulder the responsibility for realizing the great rejuvenation of the Chinese nation, and live up to the expectations of the Party, the trust of the people, as well as of this great era.[1]

"Over the past 100 years, the Chinese youth have actively participated in the great cause of the revolution, construction and reform led by the Communist Party of China, with enthusiasm for the people and the motherland. They have been fighting for the people, dedicating themselves to the motherland, striving for their happy life, offering their prime time and writing magnificent songs of youth one after another. Practice has fully proved that the Chinese youth are the ones with lofty ideals, ambitions and great creativity, and are deeply attached to their country! In the past, at present and in the future, they have always been and will be the vanguards of the great rejuvenation of the Chinese nation!" [2]

In May 100 years ago, in the face of the survival problem of their country and nation, a contingent of patriotic youth stepped bravely forward, although they were pent up in poverty, shame and grief.

The wheel of history is rolling on. China today faces new opportunities and challenges. Today's youth are striving to build a moderately well-off society in an nall-

---

[1,2] "Speech by Xi Jinping at the 100th Anniversary of the May 4th Movement ", *People's Daily*, 30 April 2019.

round way, to accelerate the building of a modern socialist country, and to realize the Chinese Dream of the great rejuvenation of the Chinese nation.

(II)

Summarizing the history and reviewing the past 100 years, we can proudly say that the 70 years since the founding of New China is a duration of earth-shaking changes in China and a great duration in Chinese history. Looking toward the future, in what dimensions and methods shall we think of the youth's values and position their mission?

The advent of any great era must have its logic. What has happened to China in the past 100 years?

From the May 4th Movement to the founding of the Communist Party of China, from the birth of New China to its becoming the world's second largest economy, from its destitution to economic take-off, especially since 1978, Chinese young entrepreneurs have support the Chinese economy to reach one new height after another. Meanwhile, these young entrepreneurs have been actively practicing corporate responsibility and promoting social progress.

From now to the middle of this century, our generation, aged from 20 to 50, is just in the prime. As the backbone of realizing the Chinese Dream, we should shoulder both the responsibility of the times and the historic missions, and contribute to the Chinese Dream -- great rejuvenation of the Chinese nation.

This book, as a masterpiece of young entrepreneur Wen Zeping, is a summary of his own entrepreneurial journey and his global vision, as well as a way to spread his positive energy.

In 2007, Wen, a post-80s young man from a poverty-striken mountain village in Dazhou, Sichuan, China, was admitted to the School of Business Administration of Sichuan University. Shortly after, he, at age 19, decided to start his business. He spent seven-to-eight hours a day on calling in a booth in his university and borrowed more than ¥ 380,000 in four months from 118 people, from ¥50 to ¥10,000. With this first sum, he became a "collegian swineherd". The road to start a business was fraught with twists and turns instead, yet he never thought of giving up. "There is no desperate situation, but a desperate mentality." He once slept in the park and had noodles with "laoganma" (a kind of sauce -- translator) for dinner. Today, his Blue Pride Media has developed from a small shop of less than 50 square meters into a strong modern enterprise.

Wen Zeping has been a self-development star of Chinese college students, one of the top ten leaders of Sichuan's new economy, and of the top ten outstanding young entrepreneurs across China. He is also a young entrepreneur who has been frequently praised by many international media as a "Name Card of China's Youth". In 2017, he donated ¥16 million to his Alma Mater, Sichuan University, and set up the "Zeping Self-improvement Scholarship" and the "Creation and Innovation Fund" for college students. He was the youngest one on the list of the 2018 Hurun Charity and Forbes Charity of all time.

As China Youth Daily commented, "From a poor mountain boy to a well-known young entrepreneur, Wen Zeping has experienced an eventful life as every hero does in novels."

Wen made a summary of himself. He thanked all the people who helped him during his entrepreneurship. "It was the 118 people who lent me money, gave me the courage and motivation to start my business. It was the Central Committee of the Communist

Youth League of China and the National Students Association that conferred me one of the "2008 Chinese University Student Self-Strengthening Star Models". It is my fellow colleagues who have accompanied me all the way."

We have to admit that a great career lies first in the education of people. In the Changjiang river the waves behind drive on the those before. Each generation produces its own talents. Only by educating youth with virtues and culture can the new generation shoulder the responsibility of rejuvenating the nation and realizing the Chinese Dream.

Wen, as a pacesetter of the new age, shoulders the responsibility for national rejuvenation, places his ideal and belief in a key position, and internalizes the spirit of patriotism and the spirit of the times with reform and innovation. He keeps his original aspiration at heart, bears in mind his mission, and helps promote the realization of the Chinese Dream by adhering to his self-confidence in the socialist road, theory, system and culture.

The core socialist values are the common values pursued by all the people. They must play the leading role in cultivating new people of the era. To button properly the first button of life, it is necessary to take education of values as a compulsory course in life.

Today, Wen Zeping's life experience, as we have seen, is nothing but the best embodiment of the responsibility of a new pacesetter in this era.

Since he achieved his phased success of entrepreneurship, he has been spreading his positive energy to the world and shared his true feelings: "Bear in mind where I started, march on with gratefulness, aim far, and be down-to-earth." When be-set with frustrations and setbacks, he never forgot his pursuit of dream. This spirit of struggle deeply rooted in his heart has influenced and inspired many others.

Wen says that he has been telling a story, his own story, and interpreting a self-strengthening spirit. “I hope that more people will regain their original aspiration, live up to their time, see where their dreams are, find their own goals and keep on fighting for them. Never give them up at any time or under any circumstances.”

With rich feelings, this book is dedicated to the young people all over the world with a hope that every reader can see the strength of this Chinese young entrepreneur from his journey, and that the youth across the world will follow his example.

Liao Yujing,

full-time writer with the Chinese Writers Association,

August 26, 2019

A Chinese dream
(Foreword II)

From its population of 540 million at the founding of New China in 1949 to that of nearly 1.4 billion today; from its expressway mileage of 19,000 km in 2001 to that of 140,000 km by the end of 2018; from its mastery of two bombs and one satellite to its success of manned spaceflight; from its access to the Internet to the being of a globally unified 5G standard; and from its establishment of Xiong'an New Area to its support of Shenzhen as a pilot demonstration area – an imposing picture of various colors has been taking shape across the 9.6-million-square–kilometer China.

Undoubtedly, the strength of any country comes from its people, especially the younger generation. The future of China and the Chinese nation belongs to its youth.

Li Dazhao, one of the CPC founders, once said that young people should "gladly devote their time to civilizing the world, creating happiness for mankind, and filling their families, the country, the nation, the humanity, the planet and the universe with vigor and vitality." The wheel of the times keeps rolling forward, and the youth remain the vanguard of the great rejuvenation of the Chinese nation either in the past, the present, or the future.

With the wind rises the clouds, the tide favors the East.

In this very extraordinary year of 2019, which marks the 100th anniversary of the May 4th Movement and the 70th anniversary of New China's birth, I have written *Youth and Dream: Struggle as a Belief*, to show how I have never yielded to my fate despite twists and turns in entrepreneurship from age 19; to show how I have been releasing my youthful passion for my dream as a young Chinese; and how I have got to know and view the world in the capacity of a "Chinese name card for youth". With great sincerity and warmth, I'd like to dedicate this book to every counterpart across the world, hoping that we can work hand in hand, sing in one voice and direct our strength for a youthful future.

The strength of the youth precedes that of the country, their independence that of the country, their freedom that the country, and their progress that of the country. Since the founding of New China, the seven-decade historical torrent has brought the motherland earth-shaking changes, which is undoubtedly the result of the great efforts made by generations of Chinese people.

We are now closer than at any other time in history to the achievement of the great goal of rejuvenating the Chinese nation. In this great new era, all Chinese youth should share the responsibility given by the times, make a plan for their life and create history.

Youth of every generation have own chances and opportunities. As young Chinese entrepreneurs, we should display our youthful power to the world. In response to the call of General Secretary Xi Jinping at the Asian Civilization Dialogue Conference, I have founded, together with my friend Liao Yujing, China Civilization Development Foundation, Asian Civilization Culture Media Co., Ltd., and launched "Asian Plan 100". We have been striving to be the inheritors and champions of Asian Civilization, to create a better future for it and even world civilization, and to write a new chapter for this era with more young peers.

At the same time, youth should always be clear that patriotism tops all. Dr. Sun Yat-sen once said that the greatest thing about being a man is to know how to be patriotic. It is not just a slogan, but a hearty feeling and responsibility. It is the deepest and most lasting feeling in the human world. Born on this soil, one should protect, love, do everything possible to make it better. I think this is the inherent mission and responsibility to every Chinese.

All Chinese youth, wherever they were born or come from, have something in common, hobbies and dreams, for example.

Some youth may still be caught in the identity dilemma - who am I? Is this really a problem? The youth, whether in Hong Kong, Taiwan, Beijing or Shanghai, Chinese or their compatriots overseas, whether they have been educated in English or Chinese, all have the same Chinese root. Emotions connected by blood, no matter when and no matter where, can never be separated.

On the axes of time and space, only we Chinese nation can boast an unbroken history of more than five thousand years up to now and trace the past in its civilization that has been inherited and passed down to the present and look to the future. When the Tang Dynasty was in its prime, its Capital City of Chang'an witnessed a galaxy of mer- chants from all countries, showing its leisurely self-confidence and broad-mindedness; and the vivid Song Dynasty painting of *The Riverside Scene at Qingming Festival* shows the metropolitan prosperity and splendid development of industry and com- merce. However, we have also experienced backwardness due to the closed-door policies, which led the feudal Ming and Qing Dynasties to their loss of opportunities for modernization. From its modern history of humiliation, the Chinese nation has come with a start: Backwardness means vulnerability to be attacked. The founding of New China shows that we have found the socialist road with Chinese characteristics. Bearing in mind our history and striving for national prosperity, we have covered by leaps and bounds what has taken the developed countries for hundreds of years.

Splendid Chinese civilization of five thousand years, humiliating modern history of over one hundred years, and reform and opening up of above forty years constitute the historical co-ordinates of the nation's inheritance and struggle. With knowledge of the past, we are clear about what lies in the future. In the contrast between time and space and the dialogue between history and reality, we must identify our own position and be sure of our responsibility. To understand the Chinese history and adhere to its cultural gene, we should always closely link our future and destiny to those of the country. This is what this book is meant to convey.

Owing to the launching of "Shenzhou-10" manned spacecraft, and "dragon" manned submersible's deep-sea diving, China today is no longer what it was! Each of us has witnessed the prosperity of the motherland and benefits from its own strength.

This is the era for talented people. The responsibility and glory of the times belongs to the youth, who are required to build the socialist modernization and strive for the great rejuvenation of the Chinese nation. Therefore, all Chinese youth are to work together for this very grand goal.

Wen Zeping

August 26, 2019

Part I

View of life: Self-awareness Decides Destiny

“ **In the face of all blows, not bending low, it still stands fast, Whether from east, west, south or north the wind doth blast.**

Bamboos amid Rocks, Zheng Xie of the Qing Dynasty. ”

If Ren Zhengfei, since he came into this world, had been complaining about the turmoil of war and the challenges facing his motherland's construction period, and the food problem of his family of eight, then there would not have been the birth of his Huawei. If Chu Shijian had chosen to beat a retreat in the face of his father's early departure and his siblings to be fed, we would not have witnessed this very king of cigarettes nor of oranges now. A look at the 21st century today presents no lack of ordinary people around us making extraordinary achievements in their own fields. In addition, a closer observation shows that they may have accumulated wealth, gained success in their life careers, or won respect and praise...

Happiness comes from hard struggle. A person may have restricted birth, but not restricted vision. There is a saying that "the sky is the ceiling," meaning that only the sky is the top, and the universe is the boundary. However, the universe is so vast and endless. Can it have any boundary? The answer is no.

Whoever you are and whatever you do, the first thing for you is to dare to think, because you cannot fly far enough unless you have an ideal high enough. Zhuang Zi said in his *Happy Travel*, "There is an enormous fish in the north sea called Kun, which is thousands of miles long, and then called Roc as it becomes a bird with a back of thousands of miles in length. When it soars, its wings seem like clouds hanging from the sky."

A fish can swim thousands of miles and turn a bird flying skyward. Then, what about you the youth? How long ago did you break through your own thinking? Have you ever changed yourself for your ideals, or even endured loneliness and poverty? Have you tried your best even when doing a trivial matter in pursuing your dream? If we ask ourselves, the answer can get plain enough.

The society today is a fair one in which the fairness is reflected in the pain and gain everyone gets. Hard work may not necessarily make you rich, but lack of it will surely keep you from it. If you cannot become a billionaire like Ma Yun, you can stay as who you are, and if you cannot be the center of the world, you can still be the center of yourself.

01 Birth: Spiritual Poverty & Material Poverty

No one can deny what he is born with, for it comes along with his birth. Few people in the world are likely to be born with a golden spoon in their mouth. We may all have an ordinary origin, an ordinary past, but nothing can prevent us from becoming who we want to be.

"With a confident life span of two hundred years, I can swim three thousand miles ahead," (by Chairman Mao Zedong -- translator). Restricting yourself where you are, you will never break free. It is always up to you to decide the destination of your life. When you intend to break through the constraint of the past, just put a full period to it, jump out of the prison of your mind, and set sail.

Birth Can't be Chosen, but Struggle Can

Our birth cannot be chosen. Some people are born rich and can enjoy wealth ever since, while others may be born poor and have to struggle on the fringe of survival. This very difference in birth is a fact.

None of us can deny our origin. In face of poverty and suffering, do you choose to retreat, escape passively, or face the difficulties and meet the challenges instead?

Like Che Yin of the Western Han Dynasty and Kuang Heng of the Jin Dynasty, youngsters hundreds of years ago have been passing on their unyielding spirits through their own experiences.

Time flows. Even though Fan Zhongyan of the Song Dynasty experienced his father's departure and his mother's remarriage at age two, he never abandoned himself. He could hardly be well fed, but stayed up late and studied assiduously as usual, going to bed with his clothes on for five long years. Sometimes he felt tired out at the dead of night, he splashed cold water on his face to stay awake. Later he turned out to be a master of Confucian classics, and determined to do something great for the world.

In his "On Yueyang Tower", he expressed the idea of "being the first to worry about the state affairs and the last to enjoy oneself," which lays bare his ambitions in life. What if one is born poor? So long as he has a lofty ideal, dares to struggle and does not give in to poverty, his life will be bright in the end.

Since ancient times, no poor backgrounds have been able to limit a person's life. If one denieshimself, and even takes poverty as an excuse for refusing to struggle or work laboriously, he has nothing but a negative and decadent outlook on life.

Huawei's founder Ren Zhengfei was born very poor and struggled for survival,and throughout three-year difficult years (1959-1962), and the "10-year Cultural Revolution (1966-1976)", and the arduous construction of New China. The outside world has even described him as a hero of untold sufferings. However, it is such a miserable origin of his that has made him exceptionally perseverant. He knows very well that, to change his status quo, the original vitality of "living on" must be kept on. This is also the strongest driving force for Huawei to become a great company.

Birth is always something past. What it can determine is the starting point but nothing ever after. Rely on ourselves and we can most probably reverse the chess of life.

It must be said that poverty, as for me, is sufferings of a sort. I come from a needy family in a small mountain village in Xuanhan County, Dazhou, Sichuan. Can you imagine that in my childhood, my family cooked each meal in a pot hung from a beam with a rope. Life was so hard, not to mention any cultural entertainment like watching cartoons. Because of this, I was the one being ridiculed by others in the village.

It is undeniable that this kind of poverty-stricken life made me, feel inferior to others for quite some time at that young age. In those days, the school in the village started from the third grade. My father had to show me how to read and write with a bar of black charcoal. Later, I went to school in the county. I could not come up to any of my fellow students, either in height, appearance, or learning skills.

Born in poverty, but I never complained . It was in face of such a condition that a sense of keenly felt self-improvement began to take root in my heart. Although I was the youngest and the shortest in class, I was eager to excel others and longed for being the top student. As I grew older, my innermost thought of ridding myself of inferiority and bidding farewell to poverty got stronger and stronger.

Urged by this spiritual power, I viewed reading as the most effective way to change my situation. The biggest gap among people has never lain in their IQ or EQ, but in their determination to keep on. I have had a very good academic record since I was young, not because of any natural endowments on my part, but the family background that once made me feel inferior.

In the presence of poverty, do you see it as an obstacle in life, or a booster for your success? In the process of growth, we should gradually learn to deal with problems dialectically. Shouldn't you consider failure as a sum of wealth, when having gone through it repeatedly in life, once you look back at it?

Poverty covers a lot. As far as birth is concerned, I always hold the view that poverty is a disaster but a piece of wealth as well. By disaster, I mean that your living environment was unoptimistic when your birth started; while wealth lies in the fact that this external environment can steel an individual to never bow his head and dare to declare war on poverty. You can't choose poverty, but you can choose to fight against it. This can also apply to a country.

It is nothing terrible that a country is poor and backward for a time. What is truly horrible is that the people of this country have long been accepting the reality of staying poor and backward without knowing how to catch up with others. As this goes on, it is not long for it to come under attack and be bullied.

In December 1959, Mao Zedong commented on what he was reading, "It is justifiable for China to be belittled, because we are not capable enough. In a big country as such, there is only so little steel, and the people's living standards are so low. In addition, there are so much illiteracy. Being looked down upon can do us good and force us to work harder and make greater progress." [1] The China then, in his words, was "poor and blank".

This has never discouraged working people or made them give up but inspired their endless fighting spirit instead. With the spirit of self-reliance and hard work, they have forged ahead despite hardships and difficulties and gradually lifted their motherland out of poverty and backwardness.

Nowadays, through decades of development, especially since the reform and opening up, China has undergone a series of great changes that has amazed the world. With its rapid economic development and continuous improvement of the overall national strength, it has not only solved the most basic feeding problem, but also stood back at the center of the world stage. In this regard, I am deeply proud of being a youth Chinese in this new era.

As the current main force of society, that is, the younger generation, if we intend to make a difference and completely break the poverty-stricken situation, we must change our mindset and disregard any individual origin and external environment as an obstacle to our progress.

---

[1] Quoted from Liu Zhengmiao, "Ideal and Reality: A Perspective on Understanding Mao Zedong's View of Socialism", *Journal of Hunan University of Science and Technology*, Issue 5 of 2013.

What Belief & What Life

"What masters the body is the heart." What inner belief brings about is the altitude of life and the life career.

A person's life has three major props, namely, value orientation, attitude towards life, and expectation. On the long road of life, some people stay restricted to life; some accomplish nothing and remain mediocre; but more are fearless as they strive for what they want to be. The key to the way of life of an individual, just like the future of a country, is whether each of us has his own ideal and belief.

In the 20th century, when China was fraught with internal and external troubles, the Communists, with a firm belief, led the broad masses to overthrow the three mountains and established the People's Republic of China. At that time, New China was still poor and weak, and it was the great decision-making of reform and opening up propelled the rapid development of China's economy and achieved the rapid increase in its comprehensive national strength.

The destiny of the individual is the same as that of the country. For all of us, especially the youth, who we want to be and what life we want to have depends on how we think about our life.

Undoubtedly, human life can often be accompanied by wealth or poverty, but can either of them really determine our life? Absolutely not.

As we all know, internal factors are the basis for the development of things. If you compare them with life, the truth is the same. As I believe, a person's birth and his material possession are important, but the more important thing is his inner belief, which largely determines his ideal and vision for the future.

May I ask whether you have ever dreamed of your future? Is there a blueprint for you to keep and strive for, or only mediocracy because you stay trapped in poverty?

Will you dash forward with your dream, or rest content with what you have now?

In fact, human life is rich and colorful, and the world is boundless. Only by cultivating our inner wealth and establishing correct values can we usher in a wonderful life.

Value orientation determines the direction of life.

General Secretary Xi Jinping once said, "Because the value orientation of the youth will decide that of the entire society in the years to come. It is very important to offer some guidance to young people when they form and establish their values in their prime. That reminds me of something that happens in our daily life. When we button up our coat, we may advertently put the first button in the wrong hole, and that will result in all the others being put in the wrong places. That's why we say that young people should "button up right" in the early days of their life."[1]

The button of life and the value orientation of the youth are closely related to the inner belief. The cultivation of a person's inner beliefs comes partly from the varied education he received from childhood. Contemporary parents attach great importance to their children's cultivation of "skills", such as music, chess, calligraphy and painting, Olympiad math and article writing. However, in the process of fighting for the goal, the most fundamental element is the spiritual power of ideals and beliefs.

However rich a country is, its people will feel like being in the desert unless they are propped by the cultural power of positive energy.

Lu Xun once said, "Since ancient times, China has no lack of people who bury themselves in hard work, who work like a horse, who plead for the people, and who bravely die for the truth." Likewise, we have never been in shortage of inner wealth.

---

[1] "Xi Jinping's Speech at the Peking University Teacher-Student Symposium", *Guangming Daily*, 8 May, 2018.

The ancient Chinese civilization, with its long history of 5,000 years, and spiritual culture of noble-minded people, are the treasures for our country and nation. For each of us, unless there are correct values as a basis and for guidance, human life is like a lone boat at sea without a compass.

Through my life journey of more than 30 years, I have jumped out of the shadow of my family's poverty and entrepreneurial failure by polishing and cultivating a strong inner world. As I look back now, the so-called power owes a lot just to my correct value orientation, which plays a positive leading role.

The attitude toward life determines the path underfoot.

Whether you were born poor or wealthy, whether you own or lose wealth, whether you meet with success or failure, it doesn't matter much.What really matters is the attitude you have at that moment.

I believe that, as one of the contemporary young people, the attitude each of us holds to life concerns the future of our country. If it is full of vigor and hope, we will be confident in dealing with any situation, and our country will be full of hope.

I have determined since my boyhood, to rid my family of poverty one day and even bring changes to my mountain village in the future.

However, what could I do at that time when I was still young? I could do nothing but study like crazy, because reading was the only way to change my life. Facts prove that even if you have nothing to your name, you can still be passionate about life when you turn the temporary poverty into a driving force for learning.

"I hope you, my dear youth, will stay young until your last breath." This is what Li Dazhao remarked many years ago, hoping that they would remain passionate forever. As time goes by, we youth of the new age have met other opportunities, and our enthusiasm and positive attitude toward life have always been with us.

A youthful dream can help you realize your ideal. How far can we go in life? The inner belief is the key factor to determine the scope of our life. "Whoever aims not for much gets some of it; whoever aims for some gets a little of it; and whoever aims for a little gets little of it." Those who are ashamed of talking about their dreams in this era will most probably get their enthusiasm wiped out by day-to-day monotony.

Your starting point may never be high. because of family poverty and lack of appearance, you probably have felt inferior for a long time since your childhood. But what will you do in such conditions? You're to stand on your own legs and follow your dreams rather than abandon yourself.

For a long time, I am glad that I have been on the road to struggle. My dreams have changed my course of life. Even through the twists and turns, I have been bravely forging ahead. I believe that, at any stage or in any situation of life, people need to have ideals. While pursuing our dreams, each of us will grow into a brave and strong gladiator, a warrior with a bright and open mind.

On our road of life, value orientation, attitude towards life and ideals are all lifelong treasures. With what kind of inner belief, we will achieve what kind of life in the future, which represents the future of our motherland.

Ordinary & Extraordinary

For a long time, people have their own criteria for judging what is ordinary and what is extraordinary. What do they refer to? What is the relationship between the two? Briefly, extraordinary flowers rely on the watering of ordinary sweat, and what is extraordinary resides with plenty of what is ordinary.

Everyone lives an ordinary life, which is the normal state of human life. in the face of the long river of history, everyone is just an ordinary person, and however glorious one is, however much wealth one owns, he is ordinary after all in comparison with the vast and unlimited time and space. Likewise, a person's life experience, even if fraught with ups and downs, it is composed of countless ordinary moments when it is divided into pieces.

Being ordinary does not mean mediocrity, nor does it mean passivity, so it can be no excuse for numbing oneself and refusing to make progress. Like most people, you may have an ordinary birth, ordinary look, and even the project you start doing is also ordinary. All in all, you may be an ordinary person who does ordinary things.

In my entrepreneurship, all vicissitudes and tastes in life filled each of my ordinary steps. In the past 12 years, every industry I have been involved in has had its good or bad markets, and my business has made a profit or suffered a loss. However, in the final analysis, it boils down to the word "ordinary". In each of the 365 days and nights, my entrepreneurship has been so ordinary. However, upon the accumulation of time, at a certain moment, the quantitative changes may bring its qualitative change, resulting in an extraordinary harvest.

In 1932, the famous Japanese industrialist Inamori Kazuo was born in Kagoshima. At the age of 23, he graduated from Kagoshima University, a second-rate medical university in Japan. Similar to the experience of most people, he is just an ordinary contry boy and attended an ordinary university. Right after his graduation, he met the Great Depression (1929-1933) sweeping across the globe and went to work in a porcelain factory. However, due to its extremely low profits, the staff could not even receive their wages, so his colleagues quitted one after another. In spite of some twists and turns, Inamori Kazuo remained and worked hard at R & D. What he did was still something ordinary. He just lived and worked in the workshop, in company of ceramics, reading magazines, learning about the latest developments in that industry, and doing experiments, day in and day out. He needed to develop the forsterite, but what challenged him most was the way to bond them together.

One day, the rosin he had kicked over glued to his trousers quite by chance. In an instant, he found the best glue. The moment when the quantitative change produces a qualitative change, his efforts for each ordinary day and night have received extraordinary returns.

Of what is ordinary and extraordinary, neither one can be judged superior to the other. They are closely related to and supplement each other. When you insist on doing an ordinary thing for a long time, you will be extraordinary one day in the eyes of others.

I often recall the hardships as I started my business. When I got out of the university, I had only one thing with me – a huge amount of debt. At that time, I still wanted to restart my business. I got ¥10,000 in return for an inspiring speech, and ¥ 5,000 in cash from my friends. Totaling ¥ 15,000 was all I had at that time. From one person to around one thousand staff, from the 50-square-meter Digital store to the current base camp of more than 6.66 hectares, the success of my business owes to my insistence for numerous days and nights.

At the onset of our entrepreneurship, we had noodles cooked in plain water spiced with "laoganma"; we squeezzed ourselves in a 50-square-meter house and sleptd in one wide bed for quite a few people. Despite such conditions, it was my long insistence on doing what I thought meaningful with a group of people that brought about the present wealth together.

In fact, every one of us is very ordinary every day, but when ordinary things are accumulated through insistence, we will sooner or later become extraordinary as others see us. A person will have some proud moments, but more often remain ordinary. If one considers himself too extraordinary and thinks himself a hero and a success, it shows that he is ignorant of what his true life is. For one, it is important to recognize that he is nothing but ordinary. Only after that knowledge of himself that can he be what he really is.

Each contemporary youth should have an ordinary mindset and be aware that each of us and everything we do are nothing but ordinary., Being ordinary does not mean that we should remain content with what we have, be lazy and slovenly, but keep our original heart for this very era, and guard against any impetuosity and depravity.

No matter how much wealth is accumulated or how many honors are bestowed on us, we are ordinary people. I do not believe in going beyond what is ordinary, nor do I agree to rest content with it. Bearing our aspiration in mind while struggling on is the proper state which shall be maintained by our generation of youth.

To achieve a great cause, we must start with small things. Being extraordinary refers more to the result of the constant accumulation of quantitative changes in day-to-day trivial things. What is ordinary can breed greatness. There is nothing superior or inferior in what everyone does, and the only difference lies in the social divisions of labor. In ordinary positions, everyone is doing ordinary things. When a person does things in a down-to-earth manner, and then gets all his ordinary moments woven, they may constitute an extraordinary moment.

The famous philosopher Zhou Guoping once said, "The Chinese people has a very simple standard. They divide the eras in history into the peaceful and the troubled ones. When the world is ruled, the people can live a happy and ordinary life; when the world is in war, or corrupt officials run rampant, the ordinary life and work get destructed." From this point of view, China is now in the former.

The peaceful and secure life we enjoy now has been created by our ancestors and countless ordinary people. At every moment, the sentrys on the border, firefighters running into the fire, angels in white (nurses) on duty, bus drivers griping the steering wheel, and so on, are all silently creating extraordinary achievements on their ordinary posts.

As contemporary youngsters, we must persist in making extraordinary achievements at ordinary positions, live up to this era, and contribute to the realization of the value of life and the great rejuvenation of the Chinese nation.

Birth & Dreams

Everyone has his dreams and pursuits. The dream of Mao Yisheng, the founder of modern bridges in China, was to be a good bridge builder for his people. This young Chinese, who came to this world when the Chinese nation was being humiliated and slaughtered, took on the responsibility of national prosperity and rejuvenation since childhood, and helped to prop China by constructing bridges.

In 1911, Mao was admitted to Tangshan Road Mine School (now Southwest Jiaotong University), a famous engineering school then. In that same year, the Revolution of 1911 broke out. He had once wanted to abandon his pen for the sword. Later, he heard Dr. Sun Yat-sen's "developing resources, setting up factories and carrying out large-scale machine production. Developing industry, prospering the market, expanding the trade,... all these are inseparable from transportation. We need to build a railway of 100,000 miles, so our hope is placed on you now."

"Building modern bridges for the motherland and letting the railway and highway unimpededly cross the rivers" had become Mao's dream ever since.

To achieve that dream, Mao developed a set of effective learning plans. When his fellow classmates were at a loss of how to learn English without regular textbooks but frequent exams, he did all in an orderly manner by jotting down the key notes from the lectures he had attended, recording and rearranging what he had read from the foreign books, and previewing new lessons after class. In many an exam, he always ranked first.

Later, while studying abroad, he was deeply concerned as usual about the motherland from across the ocean, cherishing his dream of bridge building on his return. On

December 14, 1919, he got more than passionate about his homeward ship, vowing that all his knowledge and talents would be dedicated to the motherland, in which his dream took root.

As times goes on, the present will turn into the past and the future into the present. To succeed, you must hold on to your dreams andtake efforts for their realization. The future is here, when the door to success has opened, why don't you ignite your dreams?

Everyone should have his own dreams. No matter how far the dream is from the reality, there is a possibility of materializing it. Because of the great power of dream, we can give birth to flowers of success.People can become outstanding and eye-catching just because of their dreams. Those who are devoid of such aspirations resemble but walking corpses. People with dreams are more hopeful about life.Different lives can be found with different types of dreams.

I have experienced four college entrance examinations, and each, as a dreamy journey, failed to satisfy me. I once thought that even I were 50 years old, I would go to Peking University to study literature. But the problems lie before my very eyes: One of my kinsfolk was critically ill; the only savings in the family was used up; and I was then 19 years old, the age for relieving the family of its burden. In 2007, I finally attended the Department of Business Administration, Sichuan University. Now, recalling those years, I still don't regret having such an experience, because the four years had not been spent for decadency or in vain, but been a bold dance for my dream to-be. I am grateful to the younger self who was desperate and naive, and more so to the four brutal years.

Now is the time for everyone to achieve his dreams. We must unswervingly ignite our dreams and hold them fast. There is no shortcut to their realization, but only down-to-earth efforts will yield something.

Nobody's dreams can be separated from their time and country. In those days when China was backward, we were attacked and fully humiliated in addition to reparations and loss of territory. The great dream of the Chinese people at that time was to was to expel foreign enemies from China. Now, we have stood up and got rich, so the great rejuvenation of the nation is the common dream of us all.

Today, how shall we contribute to the realization of the Chinese Dream?

Dreams are the lights guiding us forward. The more beautiful the future, the more we need to make painstaking efforts. The four college entrance examinations shattered, Failed the college entrance examination four times,and wake up from the dream of entering Peking University, but I still believed that "there will come the time for the wind to break the waves." Now, I am grateful for my previous experience of those college entrance examinations, which has served as an indispensable stepping-stone for my future life.

"One must both have great ambition and make tireless efforts to achieve great exploits." As one of the Chinese youth, I owe today's achievement of mine and, the 3.0 version of the entrepreneurial blueprint in my mind to the close relationship with my dream of the past, and the closer relationship with my experiences.

Nothing good in the world can reach us of itself. From China's accumulated poverty and weakness to its prosperity today, we have relied on the hard struggle of one generation after another. To make a beautiful dream come true, we must depend on ourselves one step after another at a time. As one of the countless Chinese people, of the Chinese youth we naturally have the blood of pursuing our dreams. Why did I dare to start my business as a freshman at college? It was the experiences in my life that had laid some invisible foundations. After I suffered, got hurt, and challenged what other ordinary people had not dared to, I remained indomitable, and still kept the spirit of forging ahead.

Martin Luther King once said, "Today, I have a dream. I dream that one day the valley will rise and the mountain will go down; the crooked road will become smooth and the holy light will show itself and illuminate the world. This is our hope. I will return to the South with this conviction with which we will be able to cleave a stone of hope off the despairing mountain."

In fact, the greatness of a dream lies not in whether it can be realized or not, but in its process, the direction that it guides, and the efforts take for it, so that one, while growing up better, can do his bit for the family, society, and country.

Follow your dream if you have one. This is not just a simple inspiring quote but also a kind of pursuit for a person to be what his ideal is like. It is a valuable attitude of being responsible for life. It is also the mighty strength gathered finally by countless people with hard work for realizing the Chinese Dream.

02 Study: No Youth without Learning

“The talents can be high or low, but the only way to knowledge is learning.” Life is short. The prime time of youth is so expensive as gold. What should you start your journey of life with? Learning is the best way.

We should read thousands of books and walk thousands of miles, keeping at heart books with or without words, and bearing in mind the family, the state, and even the world affairs. There is no limit to the sea of learning. Only when you keep your mind to it while sailing can you leave a youthful mark without regret and write a worthy chapter for this era.

Youth & the Impossible

For one in his prime, what is impossible?

fatalists always blame everything external such as birth and environment, and this negative attitude toward life is at odds with the youthful vigor. When you are so young and the world is changing so fast, complaining about why you were born in a family inferior toothers’ can solve no problem.

You may only be 20 or 30 years old now, why just limit yourself to a fixed circle with too much complaint? In the few decades of life when your time is extremely precious, trying to break the impossible by doing what young people should is the most beautiful start.

Carl Marx faced the choice between further studies and employment at 17. Some people wished him to be a poet, a scientist, some hoped him to be a priest, a pastor, and some wanted him to live a luxurious life like the capitalist, but he decided his career according to his understanding of society and his consideration of life. He said, "If we choose the profession that works best for human welfare, then the burden cannot overwhelm us because it is a dedication to everyone."

Youth means breaking everything impossible. Newton, Darwin, and Madame Curie made world-renown breakthroughs at a young age. In Chinese history, there has been no shortage of such talented figures. In the Western Han Dynasty, Jia Yi became famous at a young age. At 21, he was appointed to a position of Great Scholar. Wang Bo of the Tang Dynasty could write brilliantly when he was 6. He wrote "Preface to Tengwang Pavilion" and created classical sentences such as "If you have bosom friends far, no distance can keep you apart."

For a youth, a bold fight is a youthful declaration. Lu Xun once said, "May all the Chinese youth rid themselves of cold feelings, just go ahead rather than listen to the words of self-destruction. Do things if you can and voice yourself if you can." Living in the best era, young people today must dare to break everything impossible. Go after it without any delay.

According to Marxist philosophy, we must give full play to our own subjective initiative, persist in diligent study, paddle our own canoe, minimize the adverse effects and limitations from poverty, and even turn them into favorable conditions for personal development.

The youth is always the most energetic power, just like the sun at eight or nine o'clock in the morning. Mr. Ji Xianlin once said, "Our hope is placed on you. The progress of human society is like the relay race in the sports field. The old people run the first, the middle-aged the second, and the youth the third." So contemporary youth are supposed to shoulder the heavy responsibilities and do what is promising for them.

I believe that no matter in what era, people who do not work hard and have no core competitiveness will eventually be eliminated. A person's thoughts and actions are the key against his birth. Now, when the environment is better, young people should free themselves from the external limitations, change their destiny through real and earnest struggles, realize their dreams of life, and do something meaningful to the country and society.

One day, the relay baton of the era will be handed to you. Then, dare you the young to take over the heavy responsibility and break whatever is impossible?

I decided to start my business on the 7th day of my college life without a single cent in my pocket. How was the fund to be raised? The telephone booth downstairs of the boys' dormitory of Sichuan University costed 6 cents a minute. From morning till far into night, I spent more than four months calling and borrowing from more than 400 people, with 118 agreed. In the end, more than ¥380,000 got raised. Some lent ¥10,000, and some ¥50.

Wasn't this seemingly impossible thing, after all, became possible? You the young, try it, challenge it and go beyond yourself, for everything is possible.

For a youth, you must be courageous enough to face difficulties. In this very process, some people are better liable to reconcile themselves. However, there have been no lack of people who persist till the very end.

In the past, the ancestors shed their blood across the land and established our New China. Their youthful courage has gone down in history forever. Every generation of youth has their own chances. When we are young, we are the main force of the era, and the courage rooted in the marrow of the Chinese nation has to be passed down by us.

There is no difficulty in the world, as long as you put your mind to it. So breakingthe impossible is not a false statement.

Today, in 2019 as we look back, the reform and opening up has been lasting for more than 40 years. From a backward country to the world's second largest economy, some people in this country have got rich first. The country first catched up with other countries it had intended to in about 30 years, and then spent about 10 years to surpass them.

Miracles last forever. China is no longer what it was, with its youth now coming into a better time. Therefore you can create an incalculable brilliance.

By meeting difficulties head on, we can bring about possibilities. How to enable a flower of hope grow out of a desperate mountain ridge? How to cleave a path out of darkness? Where is the key to an impossible road? The road to success did never run smooth, so only by breaking the impossible can one see through the clouds for the moon.

For a youth, no fear of failure is his true attitude. Before I started my business, there was no shortage of doubts surrounding me. Some people asked me how if I failed; some warned me against doing it; and some wondered what I could make out of it.

In fact, since there are so many assumptions about life, why should you bet that you would lose? When one is just in his prime time, why should he rest content with a life of stagnant water free of waves? How does he know if he can do something or not without trying?

We the young must rush to the forefront of the times and dare to break all the impossible rather than do nothing for the rest of our life. However, being young does not mean dashing forward rashly. The premise for no fear of failure is that you have to know where you should go. When I decided to start my business, I did make quite some analyses.

First of all, my feeding industry never runs counter to the law. Secondly, the industry fits in with my own experience. The third, I am so young, even if I lose, I can earn it back.

Have a clear plan for the route so that you can move better toward the goal. Some people said that I was such a daredevil as to start a business on by borrowing money, for I didn't have a cent with me. In fact, I did not act on impulse. The same is true for the younger generation. We are bold but can do things in an orderly way; we are unassuming, but pragmatic; and we are young, but not impetuous.

Adhering to the goal can make the impossible possible. Persistence is one of the magic weapons for success, but the key to the problem is not how long you can hold on, but whether you can continue to do so. I turned to more than 400 people for help, and the number of rejections increased like a snowball. If you were me, how would you decide when failures kept repeating themselves?

As a youth, you should forge bravely ahead. The more you fail, the closer you may be near success.

Every one of us must have the courage to fight, the courage to face difficulties and no fear of failure so that we can achieve a career. Each of us youth should shoulder the heavy burden and make progress, so that socialism with Chinese characteristics can be full of vitality and hope.

Lofty Ideal

Whether you can achieve a dream or not depends entirely on how you act. The difficulty in realizing it is that many people have never put it into practice, done it wrongly, or persisted not long enough. It suffices, in general, to realize a dream in three steps: An accurate and clear dream; the efficient and correct execution, and unremitting efforts. These three are indispensable to and supplement each other.

How to talk about youth if we do not have great ideals?

What does youth mean? It has little to do with age but quite with the state of life. The length for each person's adolescence is varied, so are the ways to spend it. So, what kind of youths are worth praising and sung most? The one who sets a great ideal and struggles for it.

It is the best way to interpret youth by setting a lofty ideal and fighting for it. One day when you are near your last breath and recall your youthful time, I hope that you will not find it spent in a vulgar way but made up of a string of bright days filled with dreams, struggles, and valuable stories. A life full of struggle for lofty ideals is the most beautiful one.

After four college entrance examinations, the four-year college career became another journey for my youthful dream. At that time, I was eager to become an entrepreneur. After convincing my parents, I walked passionately on the road.

Marx once said, "One step of actual action is more important than a dozen programs." Supposing that you just talk about your dream but are so reluctant to take the first step for its pursuit, it can only be an illusory one with no maiden flight.

Actions are always more powerful than words. As long as you bravely take the first step, you will get a little closer to your dream. Finally, even if the dream does not come true, you have learned a lot in the process, which will be a valuable asset that no one else can take away from you.

Undoubtedly, there are ups and downs in the process of achieving a great ideal. This is the case with my business. At that time, in order to subsidize my pig-raising business, I tried many industries such as education and training, digital communication, and home appliances. Young people should be undaunted by fatigue and move on toward their ideals.

In fact, looking back at my first venture, I was quite emotional and impulsive, not so experienced of all aspects. However, newborn calves are not afraid of tigers. It may be this kind of fearlessness that helps us open the door to entrepreneurship.

For those dreamers, passionate dreaming may count more than reason. It can quickly ignite our most primitive cravings and propel us to take this significant first step bravely. As long as we do so, the second and third steps can be far easier.

In pursuing a dream, the power of persistence is necessary. It is easy to do one thing a day but far harder to insist on it for ten years. "If a sculptor stops chipping halfway, he cannot even cut dead wood, but if he keeps chipping, he can engrave metal and stone." The reason why dripping water wears stone and the rope saws the wood is that perseverance can release great energy.

Of all the Chinese entrepreneurs, I admire Chu Shijian the most. "An old steed in the stable still aspires to gallop a thousand miles." His legendary experience tells us that even if you are in your 70s, you can still fight and start afresh. The fame of Chu's orange is not in itself, but in the mental state of Chu'sperseverance and spirit for struggle.

At first, he did not know how to plant oranges, so he started to learn everything from scratch. By reading related books day in and day out, studying and consulting experts, he became quite an expert in that field. Later, although he did not work in the fields, he knew better than most farmers about fruit trees and their problems. "If I had known nothing, I might have failed to command them. Same for every industry, as far as management is concerned, you must first be familiar with the production, or you will be beating around the bush."[1]

If you set a great ideal and fight for it with perseverance, how can your dream be far off? This is an era suitable for all dreamers. As long as you dare to do it with perseverance, you will surely live up to the era.

---

[1] Zhou Hua, *A Biography of Chu Shijian*, China Citic Press, 2016.

A big dream produces a big stage. Until now, many famous entrepreneurs still call themselves "creators", people who always dare to dream and struggle hard for it.

Now, China needs more people who are innovative in mind and in deed and can persist in their dreams. Many a trickle can make a mighty sea, and it is the countless dreamers that have held up the future of the great Chinese Dream.

Birth & University of Life

What is a university?

The opening remarks of *Book of Rites • Great Learning* is, "The way to great learning is to manifest bright virtue and to treat others as one's own family, thereby arriving at supreme goodness."

Today's university differs from the ancient "great learning", but they agree on the cultivation of "gentlemanly scholars" who own great characters and pass on noble virtues. In other words, in the new era, the significance of the university lies also in cultivating young people who can shoulder the mission of this era, and be oriented to the need of modernization, the world, the future.

No youth can go without learning. The key is that you must take a steady step and lay a solid foundation for your study. Don't give it up halfway because of your own impetuosity. Whether in studying or starting a business, being down-to-earth is the prerequisite for moving toward the future.

As a young man, how will you choose to spend your college life? The Chinese youth in history have already had an answer.

On May 4, 1919, the May 4th Movement broke out on the verge of the national crisis. This patriotic movement, with intellectuals as the vanguards and the broad masses as the participants, fully demonstrated the Chinese people's efforts to save the nation and defend their national dignity. The Chinese youth at that time had gathered the strength of the entire Chinese nation to defend the country and its sovereignty.

Today, with the rise of the Chinese nation, we will no longer suffer attack as before because of backwardness. At present when every young individual has his great opportunities, he should be more aware that only by continuous learning and being in the forefront of the world could he prevent that history from happening again.

"A country is strong because of its people, and an individual is successful owing to his learning." The younger generation is the future of the country. Only by studying hard and arming ourselves with knowledge can we contribute to the great rejuvenation of the Chinese nation.

I have chosen to display my youth through entrepreneurship, and to lay the foundation of hard work with learning. At the early days of my business, I knew so little about the relevant professional knowledge that I was at a loss for making a contract. However, since I was still at college, I had the opportunity to turn to teachers in all professions for help. Whenever I had any problem in my entrepreneurial career, they taught me solutions to it with great patience.

Learning should be a lifelong cause. A person can achieve a career only when he stays in step with the era and keeps learning.

The university is the starting point of the sound values and the creation of the future. The experiences in the university teaches and educates people, expands their thinking, and makes them more aware of the responsibility bestowed by the era and society.

In the four years of college, my entrepreneurial experience met ups and downs, quite like the plot of a novel. With challenges honing my mind, I have come up with reflections on life: stick to my aspiration, march forward with gratefulness, keep a lofty ideal, and be down-to-earth.

As the youth of the new era, we should always be grateful to ourselves, the family, the society, the motherland, and the Party. Weare not only persons of the society, with public in mind, but also ones should be with a sense of national responsibility and social responsibility.

“If the youth are strong, so will the country be.” Only when our young generation be brave enough to be the forerunners, pioneers, and contributors of the era, can we shoulder the historical responsibility and the mission bestowed by the era.

Quite a lot of people in the world idle their lifetime away. How will your life go? You shall move forward while enriching your knowledge, thinking more, and shaping your dreams. You shall clearly define your goal when in university and persevere it all along.

Someone asks the significance of university. Answers vary from person to person, but definitely, you can acquire rich resources, great knowledge, and meet more like-minded people there.

At the time beset by difficulties in business, I got aided by 11 fellow classmates. When hog cholera struck my business and my funds were used up, they voluntarily treated me to dinner every day in turn for nearly a year. Therefore, I firmly believe that when the youth are bonded together, they will have infinite power.

Entrepreneurship is a hard fight, in which a single-handed fighter will most likelyfail. However, with his friends, he will be Sure of success.

The university train a group of people with broader vision. Like-minded fellows can promote each other to a higher level. The overall environment created by the university is tranquil and natural. Just like the long period of education, it cultivates students the character of being not eager for quick success and instant benefit quietly, so that the youth can ascertain their own directions ahead.

As for me, the university has far-reaching significance. From the start of my entrepreneurial idea to the practical work, as a college student, I have experienced both the joy of earning of over one million within a year and the taste of being up to my ears in debt. The lessons I have learned in the entrepreneurship during college years, and the methods offered by the teachers have laid a solid foundation for my re-start after graduation.

This is true for the great majority of young people. You should take full advantage of the environment and resources at the university, broaden your horizons, enrich your experience, pursue your ideals with vitality, and not let the present era down.

"Riding on the favorable wind, I can overlook the mountains and rivers from above." In the context of national modernization and the progress of human civilization, the university, as a place for nurturing dreams and creating the future, plays a profound part in cultivating the youth a more open vision and a more inclusive attitude. As the young generation, we must dance in the spring breeze of the new era and work tirelessly for the great rejuvenation of the Chinese nation and the realization of the Chinese Dream.

Genuine Skills

How can young people get well-versed in genuine skills in the new era?

The answer is learning. We must both read thousands of books and travel thousands of miles. We must keep abreast with the times, constantly update our knowledge, and adapt to the requirements of the era and social progress.

There is no limit to learning, but by constantly learning and being well-versed in genuine skills can we show our youthfulness in reform and opening up and socialist modernization.

What is learning? Is it a necessary burden, a must-have, or a source of happiness for knowledge?

With regard to learning, I have got a gradual process of understanding. Because I was born in a needy farmer family, learning seemed naturally associated with the change of edstiny. Although I did not understand it well, influenced by the family and teachers, the idea of studying hard has been deeply rooted in my mind since childhood. After I got to know better at junior high, learning became an inevitable way to my literary dream. During my days of pig-raising as a university student, field practice became a teacher on my road to learning, and the society became the training ground for my study.

At every stage of life, your motivations, goals and methods for learning varies. As you get older, you will have a deeper understanding of what learning means to you. However, no matter how they change, no one can afford to stop learning.

"Live and learn, and you still have much to learn." In contemporary society, to be in step with the rapid development of society and enhance one's core competitiveness, everyone should have the resolution of lifelong learning.

For individuals, learning is something that needs being integrated into daily life, just like eating and drinking. Learning cannot be done overnight, nor can it be a specific thing to be done occasionally, but in a constant state. As long as we are clear-minded, we should learn as much as possible through various channels of information provided by external feedback.

As for the country, its learning ability can presents its soft power. A country that is good at doing so can always be closely in step with the era and constantly create new wealth, both material and spiritual.

Learning remains a lifelong matter, and the improvement of national quality is a long-term journey as well. At present, our knowledge and quality are still far from the requirements of the new era.

With the profound meaning of learning in mind, one should also know how to acquire it. “What is learned from the paper is shallow, and genuine knowledge comes only from one’s action.” , it will be in vain if reading is not combined with practice, however much you have read.

So how should one learn? Is it to learn book knowledge first and then put it into practice, do the latter while learning, or learn directly from practice?

Each of these three has its own focus and is suitable for different learning scenarios. None can say for sure that one is better than the others. While at school, we usually adopt the first way of learning. However, after graduate, the second and third ways serve individuals better for seeking real knowledge.

The truth comes from practice. Usually, various problems that show up in practice will force us to learn and summarize, and finally find solutions to them by applying theories. This process is quite painful, but helpful for us to learn a lot of real knowledge.

While raising pigs, I bought books about pig breeding, asked teachers for help or simply checked the Internet to handle the problems. I learned the professional skills of drafting a contract and vaccinating pigs. It was through my personal practice that I had become half an expert from a nonprofessional in a short period.

Learning can be done in various ways. Sitting up with a book in one’s hands is just one of them. In addition to my practice in a narrow sense, communicating with others, traveling, etc., are good ways for learning, too.

“In the company of three persons, one can serve as my teacher for sure.” As long as you feel it with your heart, everyone around you has something you can learn. In other words, each of them is qualified to be your teacher in one way or another. Perhaps, a friend at your side casually points something out to you, which will inspire you at once, or help you with a new perspective.

Traveling is also a special way of learning for self-cultivation. "It is no greater joy than feast your eyes on the great universe and all that thriving on earth. they will gladden and broaden your mind and heart." On the way, the beauty of nature and humanity will give you visual enjoyment and spiritual comfort. This silent internalization can continuously enriches you and expands your vision and mind.

Of course, this does not mean that reading and studying is unimportant. No matter how you are pressed for time, you should make use of the piecemeal time for books, newspapers or the latest news through the new media. Recently, while preparing for China Colorful Civilization Development Foundation, I have made a targeted reading plan with my friends.

As the messengers, inheritors and champions of Chinese civilization and even Asian civilization, we must familiarize ourselves with the history and civilizations of China, Asia and even the world, so as to speak for China and Asia and do our share to spread Chinese and Asian civilizations globally.

In the report to the 19th CPC National Congress, the construction of a learning-oriented society, a learning-oriented political party, and a learning-oriented power has been proposed as an important task for the Party and the country. In the process of accelerating the construction of a learning-oriented society, we the contemporary youth must be well-versed in genuine skills, enhance our ability for learning, be brave in practice, and constantly innovate and strive to enhance the core competitiveness of individuals and the country.

Constant learning for genuine skills is the only way for young people to achieve success. Today, we contemporary youth are required to jump out of our own limited thinking and observe problems from a higher perspective. Only by sharpening this sense of urgency and advancing with the times for new knowledge can we contribute our youthful strength to the socialist modernization.

03 Entrepreneurship: Situation & Mentality

When Winston Churchill made a speech at Oxford University, he mentioned three secrets of success: The first is never to give up; the second is never, never to give up; and the third is never, never, never to give up!

No one can be carefree and undisturbed throughout his life. He may have some difficulty at school, be frustrated in work and come across some enforseen events in entrepreneurship. desperate situation will not turn away from you. Only when you never stay in despair nor give up, will you have the possibility to start afresh.

Power of Belief

The result leading to the belief, or the belief leading to the result -- these are two entirely different sights. As far as entrepreneurship is concerned, once something is proven correct, it is no longer at its primary stage, so you can't share the market dividend with people who have believed in it. In other words, you are only one of those spectators in front of majestic mountains and rivers.

Seeing it because of believing is another feast of resources and wealth provided by the mountains and rivers.

Over a decade ago, there was a small and medium-sized Chinese bank with only a few hundred outlets, which seemed impossible to match any of the four major state-owned ones in a short period by opening more outlets. Yet its leader firmly believed that Internet banking could change the traditional banking industry, and retail banking would be the future of that industry. At that time, utilizing whatever resources possible, they opened nine branches across the country, and invented the so-called All-purpose

Card with new technology to replace the traditional passbook. It is called China Merchants Bank and Ma Weihua is that leader.

Ma believed that China's credit card era would come. At that time, all the world's leading consulting organizations thought that the credit card would find no market in China, and the Chinese would not embrace the era of early deficit spending.

Ma, so sure that China's credit card would do otherwise, got ready his China Merchants Bank in advance with his firm belief that young Chinese would grow up rapidly as the possible cardholders. In the end, his Bank released the first practical Chinese and foreign currency credit cards across China. Today you can see that its credit card is almost the leader of this kind all over the world.

From all-purpose card to credit card and to wealth management, China Merchants Bank is the most unique. It has become a banner for the banking industry not because it has got a different opportunity or a better foundation than any others. The greatest reason is that Ma and his team believed in the future of China's wealth market, and had the rest stalked by getting everything ready.

This is because he trusted in the power of "belief". A disciple once asked Buddha, "Where is the world of bliss? How can I believe when I can't see it?" Buddha led him into a room, saying, "There is a wooden fish inside here. Try to find it." That room was too dark for one to see his own fingers, the disciple said, "I can see nothing." Buddha lit a candle and the wooden fish lay in the center of the room. Doesn't it exist just because you cannot see it? In front of unknown things, people either believe because they see or see because they believe. Ordinary people believe that seeing is believing, while entrepreneurs see it because they believe.

An innovative enterprise with a fresh business model gets it doubted at first, just because such model is always breaking the old pattern of interests and the rigidness of thinking. The arrival of a new world always takes such a problem along, and some people completely negate it just for that reason.

The terrible thing is to have your view overshadowed by the trivial. For entrepreneurs, what matters is not quite your product, your industry, the external environment, but whether you really believe that you can bring values to others and whether you can succeed.

Today, on the road to realize the Chinese Dream, if you believe it because you see it, you will find it hard to move on; but if you see it because you believe it, you will have a firm belief in the Chinese Dream and have your dream connected to it. In this way, your Chinese Dream will surely be realized.

This is the best era, and Internet technology is propelling the change of our life in each passing day. Today, the speed is unprecedented for individuals to realize their dreams.

The Chinese Dream is the one for the Chinese nation to strengthen itself and the one for the broad masses to start up own business. As long as we cherish such a dream, we will get the opportunity to realize it.

The most important thing is that you must believe that it can be realized!

Choice & Struggle

What determines the individual's destiny is the power of belief and courage for a break-through. As few people reached South China in 1992, or a long time afterward, so many failed to join the economic wave of China's reform and opening up, and therefore missed that round of wealth dividend.

"The early bird catches the worm." When you are still hesitating, some others have already been on their way. They choose the general trend of history and get their opportunities in return.

What has been China's core mission for the past 40 years? It is the one centered on economic construction. In these four decades, very few artists have shown up in China. If many people have chosen art, instead of business, their life today would be far different.

Mass entrepreneurship and innovation. In recent years, the entrepreneurial trend in China has been on the rise, and plenty of individuals have been thinking about starting their businesses. Some people have failed, but the others made it. Why? Because of their different choices.

Entrepreneurship cannot be done on impulse but need be preconditioned by figuring out why you are starting your business. It may carry a tinge of passion, but what matters most is that you must be aware that it is nothing like a trend to go after. Only by clarifying ideas from the ideological level can you establish a phased plan for yourself to strive for the goal.

To some extent, every individual owns the ability to turn dreams into reality what he insists on them. As long as his perseverance and his action are strong enough, his possibility to materialize his dream from imagination to reality will be greater.

At senior high, in addition to my literary dream, the aspiration for being an entre preneur was deeply rooted in my mind. In my opinion, my entrepreneurial motivation consists of three components: creating wealth, realizing personal values, and making social contributions. At different stages of my entrepreneurship, the proportion of these three drivers was different. So, what exactly is entrepreneurship for? The answer is simple. In fact, it is to achieve the individual value and ideal of life. With many choices in life, it is too difficult to figure out what kind of person you want to be.

A reporter once asked me if I felt that I was a born entrepreneur. I shook my head.

When engaged in business, I can only say that I always choose to believe: believe in myself, and in this country.

There is no royal road to entrepreneurship. There is some inexplicable truth in sone's description of the road to entrepreneurship --"damned true love." As mentioned by this very person, the probability of a company coming to market from Round A is about 1 in 170,000. Such a low probability is so like the chance of encountering the true love.

There exists such a possibility all the time. Just try hard, and the opportunity may favor you. I am naturally optimistic. Even when I was in debt, I never forgot to encourage myself: Should I make it, I would be the youngest entrepreneur.

However, as far as entrepreneurship is concerned, you must have a clear understanding. For me, born in a poverty-stricken family, my entrepreneurship from the very beginning was solely for some changes of my living condition. It has its phased character. The university marked the first stage. When I faced the very problem of feeding myself, it served as my driving force to change the circumstances for my family so my parents could live a better life and I coulud realize my value and achieve the dream – being an entrepreneur.

Fresh from college, I started my business in debt and with the original problem of surviving. While pursuing my value and ideal, I had to strive for the status quo. Unless I solved that problem, there was not room for entrepreneurship. An ancient said, "Before your success, strive for self-cultivation; when in success, try to serve the world." As my company has gained its strength enough, practicing its social responsibility becomes a matter of course.

My value of life, as I divide, runs down to two levels. First, make the company bigger and stronger together with the employees, and assume more social responsibility;

second, call on more young people to share the national responsibility and contribute to the motherland, since I myself alone is far from strong. A person's life span is limited, so is his energy and strength. If as many people of my age as possible can be convinced to work together, the energy we can produced will be more than calculable.

I have mentioned above the reason for entrepreneurship. If you regard that as making money, you won't go far for sure.

Entrepreneurship is one of the routes to realize the value of life. It is always closely connected with the love for the Party and the country, with contributions to the society, and with the sharing of social responsibility. The motherland and the era have given us the opportunity, so it is a matter of course for us to be dedicated to the country.

Today, the youth of the new era are in the best period of the development of the Chinese nation. They face the ideals of life and the mission "to be shouldered as destined." In this new era, the Chinese youth should continue to carry forward the spirit of the May 4th Movement and fulfill the great rejuvenation of the Chinese nation. They should be worthy of the expectations of the Party and of the people, the trust of the nation, and live up to this great era.

Survival of Forerunner

Be brave enough to stand in the forefront, so that we can march forward effectively. Once you are hit back onto the beach, the game is over. It is so crucial to seize the opportunity. Without mature external conditions, however it is worth doing afresh, you should choose to give it up in time unless. If you persist in it, you will only bear a higher cost and more risk. Likewise, no matter you are promoting new products, using some new technologies, expanding new markets, or communicating with new customers, a company must act before its rival(s), by just a half step ahead, which is the best choice.

Why just a half step ahead? Because there is risk control behind it. Owing to such a half step, one can have the opportunity for development while leaving himself room for recovery as well. Any innovation has its risk. Since it is impossible to reduce the risk to zero, it is necessary to learn to control it properly.

"Move along the trend, but a little ahead of the rest, or you will have no chance; but if the step is too quick, you may slip or stumble. So a half step ahead can leave you room for moving forward or backward. When you go forward, be the leader; as you move backward, you have little to lose." With this idea of in mind, Liu Yonghao of New Hope Group, who started his business by selling quails, has turned into a leader in the agriculture and animal husbandry across China.

In the past 40 years, a lot of Chinese enterprises have had entrepreneurial experience. So many years of struggle have witnessed the leaders in various fields. They have stayed ahead of their competitors relying on advanced techniques, ideas, products, talent, management or marketing. Now, in the 41st year of reform and opening-up, when Chinese companies have entered a new stage of development, all the leading companies of the past need to think about something new: How to stay ahead and live longer?

In the Internet product community, there is a very popular term called "fast iteration", which means continuous updating, upgrading and optimizing of products. For any Internet product, its course of life is a process of constant updates from Version 1.0 to Version n.0 .

In a like manner, only an entrepreneur with the thinking of updating can help his company to stay ahead and seize every opportunity that comes in his way.

There are many choices for entrepreneurial projects. Whether it is a traditional or emerging industry, the key lies in whether it is suitable for you in terms of dynamic development. My entrepreneurial experience can fall in three periods: the breeding, the digital, and the media. Each phase has its own feature, which closely adapts to the times and leads others by a half step.

In 2007, when information was not as developed as it is today, my parents told me that quite some people had made a fortune from pig-raising in Guangzhou, Guangdong, China. Coming from a traditional peasant family, I was familiar with this trade. . Considering the possible assistance of my parents also, who were in Guangzhou as migrant workers, I deemed it worth a try based on its feasibility.

In 2011, I faced adverse conditions in pig-raising, so I turned to digital electronics. One year later the smartphone was published, followed by the era of digital entrepreneurship. In 2016, I oriented the company to the media industry and started my business.

Since I entered the college, I has involved myself in more than a dozen industries, including electronics, communications, training, farming, healthcare, culture, and media. Because of my continuous attempts and close attention to these industries, I have seen the prospects of the media industry and owned the current scale of enterprise.

All these layouts of a plan are nothing unrealistic nor groundless. Instead, they are choices that need more courage and the control of opportunities than others. At the onset of my business, my team, though deep-rooted in the traditional industry, was all the time leading the innovation. In different periods, I have different opinions on the combination of the traditional and emerging industries, such as the Internet. When I was in the digital industry, a friend suggested that I extend the industry to the Internet but I refused. During the media period, with the change of strategies, I actively embraced the emerging Internet industry . In the dynamic development of the big environment, and myself my viewpoint has changed, so has the concept of "being proper".

The selection of entrepreneurial project is complicated. It includes factors like timing, geographic convennience and human relations. I have involved more in the traditional industry, because it is very fit for me. Young entrepreneurs should also size up "being proper" when it comes to the selection of projects, instead of blindly follow the much-sought-after industries.

Every industry has its own hope, yet "what is fit for you is the best" should go through the concept, with you yourself being the dominating part. I firmly believe that, on this very planet, the human really counts.

In *The Stars of Humanity*, Stephen Zweig wrote that, "A person's greatest fortune is to find his mission at his peak in the journey of life." I think the concept of mission is to find the dream that you are willing to fight for, find the right route and the right direction to make the dream come true.

The "half step" and the fast iteration can work better based on finding the right industry fit for oneself. That is the common trait of good leaders. If one waits for the arrival of a trend and then moves toward it, he will end up lagging behind others. Only a layout in advance can help people save themselves.

Mohandas Karamchand Gandhi once said, "At first they ignored you, then laughed at you, then struggled against you, but you won in the end." This is true for the commercial society as well, where the forerunner must bear the chastening before he can become the leader of the next wave.

Chen Chunhua, a professor of management, believes that, for a company to maintain its leadership, it should possess five major capabilities: first, do things more solidly; second, have a strong sense of crisis; third, have to be worthwhile even if it fails; fourth, learn and compete; and fifth, all employees are innovative.

To strive for the leading position of an industry, the leader's vision, dream and aspiration of an enterprise matter a lot because they are the key factors that guarantee success. A transforming enterprise needs a leader because the process of change is unclear and challenging. The leader now must display his great role in leading all else toward the achievement of their goal.

Be Down-to-earth & March On

The Chinese character " 人 "(meaning a person in English -- translator) is made up of two strokes, which support each other with a head above and two feet firmly down to earth. This shows that people must always rely on each other to be steady in moving forward together.

Being down-to-earth is the premise. If a person, who is impetuous and immersed in fantasies all day, always follows a shortcut rather than practice, whatever idea is in his mind, he will accomplish nothing. To some extent, being down-to-earth is even more important than having a head filled with ideas. Any idea, however long cherished, has to be materialized eventually. Just start from the little things around you, and gradually create everything you have conceived with your own hands.

Many a little makes a mickle, as a proverb says. Throughout the ages, whoever has intended to do something great has started from something very small.

In daily life, everything a person does, good or not, is driven by his innermost thoughts and closely related to his spiritual qualities and ambitions as well. A person with a lofty ideal can get it reflected in everything he does, no matter how ordinary it is.

A person chasing his dream in a down-to-earth manner will never be impulsive or addicted to illusory fantasies from day to day, never eager for quick success or wish that his dream would come true overnight. He will just put his heart into it, start with the most trivial, perfect them.

Every minor matters brings along something extraordinary. The accumulation of trivial things such as a small habit, a small profit and a simple choice determines where you will eventually go. The smaller the detail, the more worthy of being serious.

"One cannot run a country well unless he first does his own house well." For a person who cannot handle things properly around him, what else can he do? "Cultivate individual moral character, run the family in unison, manage the nation in order, and peace will prevail throughout the universe." In addition to doing small things, one should be down-to-earth starting from very things close by, and then move on to those on a larger platform, like the family, the society, the country.

Being down-to-earth also means that you should not blindly make a plan or do anything that is far beyond your ability. Do whatever thing according to your own ability. Otherwise, not only your wish cannot be fulfilled, but also what you have done is not worth your effort.

During my startup of business at university, the pig farm I rented needed 80 pigsties. In order to save some costs, I had the help of my parents and grandfather, who was in his seventies. We four went with a tram to a garbage dump near an industrial park five kilometers away for some discarded bricks.

In this way, the four of us gathered seven or eight thousand bricks in a week. Later, we scraped off cement from the used bricks with tools and built 80 pigsties with the cement at a very low cost.

At the very beginning, I carefully calculate and strictly budget every penny. Without this spirit, I could not get so far. However, entrepreneurship does not mean to save money or force oneself to do everything. All you have to do is use the money where most needed. For what you can't do, you have to turn to a professional.

For the individual, being down-to-earth is a daily job. It can be a good word, a kind deed, and a steady step forward. Sticking to the ground, one will not miss his step and fall down on the journey, but instead can go farther for his dream.

For the country, being down-to-earth is the long journey of rise in the world, and it is a choice determined for developing by burying oneself deeply.

Today, after decades of its development and construction, China has long ceased to be what it was -- the poor, weak and backward country. Now, as the youth of the new era, we should start from the little things around us, do more solid and good ones that are meaningful to our country and society.

Courage & Struggle

Great men of any era are steeled in repeated struggles with no exception. The phoenix can gain rebirth only after its nirvana. In the same way, ionly the phoenix that stands still proudly in the fire can claim that name.

"The fragrance of plum blossoms comes only from frigid weather." To see a more beautiful scene, you must be brave enough for a fight and make corresponding efforts.

On the long road of life, setbacks never disappear. The destiny of a person is in his own hands. He must remain convinced that the sun will always rise, even if it is still under the horizon for the time being.

How to tell the strong from the weak? Very simple. Can you adjust yourself as far as you can when in the same environment and with the same mood?

The speed a person adjusts his mood is roughly the speed he gains his success. The faster you do, the more likely you are to succeed. Even in the face of the 100th failure in life, the strong can still bravely say, "As long as I stand up one more time than I am knocked down, I am hopeful for success." Some people say that every entrepreneur is a cat with nine lives. Over the years, I have been in many desperate situations and countless times on the verge of collapse, due to the fail of entrepreneurship, the betrayal of partners, the incomprehension of friends and even the loved ones, and the ridicule of others. Beset with all thses, I complained some time, and even thought of giving up. These memories made me lonely, feeling that everyone was belittling my dream and value. When I was beaten black and blue by reality, I shed tears and even thought about suicide.

However, escape can solve no problem. There is no desperate situation in the world, but only a desperate state of mind. It is said that despair is the greatest sorrow. As long as my young heart keeps beating, success will be around the corner.

In a person's youth, frustration and pain can shape his hard work and fighting spirit. When one is young, his experiences of setbacks and tests can raise him to a higher plane in addition to an indomitable will and pioneering spirit.

Learn to turn a negative emotion into a positive energy and use frustration as a test of life. This superpower shown in adversity will win the admiration of your friends and even rivals, and help you turn the table.

Ren Zhengfei once said, "The bird that won't die in flames is the phoenix. A saint is the one who can climb out of the mud pit." At the end of 2008, when the largest swine fever swept across China since the reform and opening up, my farm was not spared. Overnight, more than 200 pigs died, and the economic loss directly knocked down my unprosperous family. My parents, who could hardly accept the reality, even attempted to commit suicide in a reservoir. Fortunately, they were intercepted.

When nothing is left, the human spirit rebounds from its rapid collapse. With four failed college entrance examinations, I had put great pressure to my parents. Now my complete defeat in business almost killed them. Nevertheless, I believed as always that my destiny was still in my own hands. As a saying goes, "He laugh best who laugh last."

I comforted them that "One day I will make it." Finally, we went through that plague and raised piglets again. Everything seemed so smooth until the once-in-a-hundred-year financial crisis caught me unawares. The price of pigs tumbled all the way, from ¥ 10 to around ¥ 5. All my hopes died out like a bubble.

At this very point in life, it seemed hard for me to go any further, until the opportunity presented itself, leading me out of despair. By chance, I found that there was a huge market for local pigs in Guangzhou. I had been assuring myself that I must believe that all the unfortunate was transient. A stronger voice inside kept warning me that I could be depressed for one day or two, but not forever.

Entrepreneurship did not favored me even for a while. As everything turned for the better, my business was running out of money. In that very year, I won the honor of "China University Student Self-Strengthening Star". I went to Beijing by train for the 10,000-yuan prize, and put it all in the pig farm. To alleviate the economic pressure, my parents found jobs in a boiler room, in which they refined copper and aluminum day and night.

Misfortunes never come singly. My mother suffered comminuted fractures in both legs due to a motorcycle accident. After more than two months' stay in the hospital, she stayed at home for a year.

The broken capital chain resulted in a lack of fodder for more than 2,000 pigs. My seriously injured mother was still bedridden. I was locked in an infinite loop: I kept selling pigs and kept borrowing and paying back money. In order to close the financing gap for pig-raising, I started selling mobile phones, giving training courses, running a home appliance store, and whatever I could think of.

"All that can't kill you will eventually make you strong." From start to finish, I have never bowed to fate. After all, the road of life is made up of passes, and the passage of each means a step forward.

Of the four-year undertakings at college, all the bad things came one after another. Later, when everything dot better, I was deceived by my partner of the small appliance store and became penniless. I, only 21 in my third year at college, was so poor that even cannot pay for water. However, I still had the determination to start all over again.

For me, my first business makes an important stage for me to realize my dream, to temper my mind, to comprehend the true meaning of life, and to improve my vision of life. The reason why I was able to make a quick start after graduation owed a lot to what I had gained there. The first business was my preparatory and buffer period of life, during which I became more mature, whether in psychological quality, attitude towards adversity and honor, or interpretation of entrepreneurship. All these had laid a solid foundation for my later entrepreneurship.

Human growth follows a spiral rise rather than a straight one. In this process, adversity is the turning point and the decisive moment. Under the external pressure, you must constantly break through your own limits and find the way out of the death valley. Meanwhile, your courage and wisdom can be improved, and your mental qualities and work abilities can be exercised.

Inamori Kazuo once said, “When in failure and suffering, you should not complain or blame others, but endure trials and persist, trying to turn what is adverse into something good. When in success and luck, guard yourself against arrogance, stay grateful, remain hardworking and keep your success.”

No matter in what era, despite different spirit of the times, the main theme is always spreading the positive energy. Facing the life, we should have hope; confronting setbacks, we should challenge them. If you fall down, you must get up, fight on, and write a youthful song in a heroic tone. Facing the great era of reform and opening up, we must be spiritually indomitable to build our great motherland and realize the great rejuvenation of the nation together.

Aspiration & Dare

Measuring the world with "both legs scarred", as for Ren Zhengfei, is the truest portrayal of Huawei's progress.

In 2015, in the themed advertisement published by Huawei, a ballet dancer's feet touched people's hearts. As the photo showed, the ballet dancer's feet in dancing shoes were elegant and beautiful, while the other feet were naked and covered with scars.

"Behind greatness lies suffering." For decades, with its strong belief in continuous transcendence and its efficient and powerful combat effectiveness and executive force, Huawei has created many a first in its field and gradually grown into a well-respected and trustworthy global enterprise. All of these originates from a seemingly ordinary experience of Ren Zhengfei many years ago. In the mid-1980s, when a friend asked him to sell a SPC exchange machine, Ren saw a huge business opportunity.

At that time, China could not independently produce such a device while the West restricted exporting its technology to the Chinese mainland. As a result, many businessmen chose to get them from Hong Kong and Taiwan to resold them after relabeled. Quite some domestic manufacturers wanted to take the lead in the market and tried to break through the technical obstacles of such a machine.

After Ren's proposals of research and development of the machine were rejected time after time, Ren made a decisive resignation. In 1987, he came out of the system in his midlife, and later officially founded Huawei in Shenzhen. It is said that with a lofty ideal and the courage to act, you can see different sights in the same scene. There have always been countless Chinese people, who are courageous enough to be the first to eat crabs. They believe that the Internet can bring about disruptive innovations and can be a tool to help companies stand out in a new round of competition. Therefore, of all enterprises, China Merchants Bank took the lead in launching e-commerce, Suning Mall created an online cloud merchant, and Logic Thinking achieved an annual sales revenue of books over ¥ 100 million through the WeChat Public platform. Of the self-employers, multi-millionaires constantly emerged by virtue of the mobile Internet.

With the vast trend of the era, everyone can have a dream. The power of the spirit plays a leading role in their way.

The same is true for the road of entrepreneurship. Since human beings entered the 21st century, information technology, such as cloud computing, big data, and Internet of Things, has been bursting out. Artificial intelligence has developed rapidly. Innovation and globalization have brought unprecedented changes to the world. The enterprises' survival and development have faced different challenges from the past. In the same way, in addition to cultivating innovative talents and building innovative teams, we need to strengthen the inner strength of our team further.

"Aspiration can reach any place however far it is, even over mountains and seas; and it can break through any defense however tough it is, even as strong as the best armor and shield." The power of spirit can make people break the rules and the inherent shackles, and make people stronger through challenges.

The factors of success are diverse, and no simple conclusion is scientific enough. However, no matter how it develops, the spiritual culture buried deep inside the enterprise must not be ignored. Even in terms of human survival and development, the role of spirit can never be underestimated. Ren Zhengfei, President of Huawei, once remarked, "Israel is an example for us. The Jewish nation that has been separated for two centuries, after returning to their homeland, have created wondrous miracles in the desert where resources are scarce and severely depleted. Their resources are from their clever minds. They rely on the power of spirit and culture to create world miracles."

I often say that a past plague practically ruined all my hopes and landed me in a desperate situation with no way to go. Later, when my parents committed suicide because of the high debts, I was so depressed that I wanted to kill myself. However, whenever frustration strikes me like an avalanche, there is always a sentence supporting me -- Are you really defeated? When you are in difficulty and feel helpless, I hope that you can ask yourself likewise. Are you really defeated? For young people, to aim high requires the unremitting struggles for the great belief.

A review of the 100-year-long journey, which was under the guidance of lofty ideals and beliefs, shows that young people actively participated in the revolution, construction, and reform undertakings led by the Party one generation after another. They fought bravely, and dedicated in the main theme of the times -- standing up, getting rich, and being strong. They had written a series of youthful songs with blood and sweat.

As contemporary youths, when the good opportunities present themselves, we must bravely advance for our ideals and display our true nature. Even in difficulties, we should be aware that everything is constantly changing, and a failure is not the final.

When Chu Shijian's life was just getting better, he was sent to a farm as a rightist. When he became the king of cigarettes at the peak of his life, he was accused of corruption and was thrown into the Luoyang prison. From the bottom of the valley to the peak, he, over 70 years old, contracted for planting oranges on Ailao Mountain. Ten years of efforts made him the king of oranges. It is all owing to the power of faith.

The high aspiration of the youth is a reflection of their outlooks on life, on values and on the world. "Whoever is devoted to his career shouldn't boast of his wealth; whoever is chasing wealth shouldn't laud himself." As a young person, you must play your role well. While pursuing your ideals of life, you must not forget the interests of the motherland and the people, or the social responsibilities you should assume.

Ideals are lofty and great, but you should never ignore people who have accompanied, helped and assisted you. Whether to the company team or to partners, gratitude is crucial in the entrepreneurial process. The era of individual heroism has long passed, and the power of a single person is no longer as powerful as that of teamwork.

One hundred years ago, countless young people with the ideal of saving the country walked together. They used the power of the group to arouse the nation and defend the interests of the motherland. Now, in the journey of entrepreneurship, the partners who work together with you are the most valuable assets.

Imagine that if I had no support from my parents who quitted their jobs, from the 118 people who lent me money, or from my alma mater and my classmates, I doubted whether I could go on the road of entrepreneurship.

Be ambitious and more grateful. I encouraged my employees to be grateful to their own Alma Mater by setting up scholarships there. When they do this despite the amount of the bonus, a huge positive energy will form. Bit by bit from the company to the entire society, we can inspire more and more people.

A person is valuable only when his ideals are combined with the future of the country and the nation.; only when his pursuit is consistent with the needs of society and the interests of the people.

We are all small fractions in the river of history, and we should all be grateful to this era for what it has created for us. We should be grateful to the country, the nation and the Communist Party, because without them creating this great era, without them providing such policies and conditions, we would not have today's life. Each of us should aim high and go out with our youthful blood for the great rejuvenation of the

Chinese nation.

Era & Entrepreneurship

In the past few years, the rise of WeChat, and its combination with traditional ecommerce has birthed a flower called Microbusiness. It has been growing surprisingly fast. Who has not seen its presence on his Moments? Should time go back a few years ago, who could have expected its arrival?

The high-speed rail, scan code payment, shared bicycle and online shopping are called China's "New Four Inventions", with two obvious characteristics:

First, they have all appeared intensively in a very short period of time, far shorter than the timespan of their forefathers.

Second, they have all been concentrated on the Internet, closely related to and even dependent on each other. For the high-speed rail, without the support of Internet technology and mobile payment, it wouldn't be so convenient and speedy as it is now.

As we all know, the Internet age is an era of information explosion. When the opportunities rush toward you like a flood and one wave after another, how will you respond to them?

My answer is to embrace the era of entrepreneurship and bravely go for it. In fact, entrepreneurship seems glamorous and bright but a painful experience. The more radiant the face is, the sadder and bitter the heart is. Many people may only see the brilliance of entrepreneurial success instead of the hidden hard work of each entrepreneur.

Why was I willing to choose this suffering on the beautiful and comfortable campus? One word: dream. Since I will definitely take the road of entrepreneurship, I'd better leave for it as soon as possible.

When giving lectures at colleges, I was often asked whether they should start their business or not. My answer is: Once you have decided, just do it boldly. Do not worry about the past nor the future.

The greatest pleasure in life is that the past road cannot be retraced, and the future is still unclear. What you should do now is to get on the road boldly and be courageous to fight on.

This is a great era suitable for innovation and entrepreneurship, and a beautiful one with rewards for young people who fight for it.

China is now in the critical period of realizing the great rejuvenation of its nation and the new round of reform and opening up. The era of "mass entrepreneurship and innovation" is booming, and entrepreneurship is becoming a new employment model favored by the majority of young people.

Now, the entrepreneurial environment created by the country, society, and universities is very favorable. If you want to leave school to start a business, you can; if you want to start a business at school, there is a service center for innovation and entrepreneurship on campus; if you want to start a business after your graduation, there are entrepreneurial incubators around the world. In addition, as the whole society becomes more open and active in thinking, people's understanding of entrepreneurship is deepening; the tolerance for entrepreneurial failure is far greater.

I am very envious of the young people of the present. When I started, the entrepreneurial support was insufficient. Nevertheless, I, so poor then, had the guts to do it, what do you fear now?

Now is the best era of entrepreneurship. Various social supporting resources are getting more and more mature, various venture capital institutions are set up, the investment and financing system is increasingly perfecting, and the financial pressure of powerful entrepreneurs is smaller than ever. With the development of information, transportation, and logistics networks, information has become more efficient and convenient, and the efficiency of entrepreneurship has been greatly improved. I had to check the information of pigs at the Internet café at that time. For the young people now, whatever information needed can come to you at the moment you touch your phone.

Behind the infinite opportunities often lie infinite challenges. First of all, the competition between today's industries is getting more and more fierce. An entrepreneur without particularly good products and projects may soon be replaced.

Secondly, the operating cost for an enterprise is getting higher and higher, and the cost of rent and employment is constantly rising, which is quite a test for a start-up.

Thirdly, some business starters may rush forward just on impulse without full consideration.

In fact, I did the same in the past. Due to the poverty of my family when I was young and the experiences of four college entrance examinations, I was more independent than my peers. When one who has experienced the shaping of personality is confronted with setbacks, he will have a better ability to rebound.

Despite the many concerns, whenever someone asks me whether I should start a business, I would say that I would do it bravely without hesitation.

Failure is not terrible. It is terrible to fear failure and fail to take the first step. Pay less heed to the result, but more attention to the process, and have a mentality to embrace failure. What will happen if you fail? So long as you have a breath, just stand up and continue fighting.

As an experienced person, I want to give young entrepreneurs some advice. First, we must have the awareness of law and regulations, , and never touch anything against the law. There are many things worth doing and fighting for in life. Do not trap yourself in the illegal as a result of act on impulse and polish your eyes instead for the correct direction.

Meanwhile, never expect too much. As a greenhorn, do not aim too high, and be sure that your goal is to survive. Do not say so readily that your company will "come into the market", "turn out to be the unicorn", and so on. Surviving is of the top priority.

Second, be rational and do according to your ability. You need to objectively assess things you are able to bear and control the cost of startup within what your family and you can bear in the next 10 years. Don't go beyond this, or you may have to pay for 10 years or even a lifetime.

How many 10 years do you still have? If a round of entrepreneurship has landed you and your family into a situation where you cannot extricate yourself, just drop it as soon as you can.

Finally, fight to the end with clenched teeth. Entrepreneurship is like waking a tightrope, which entails plenty of risks. Entrepreneurs must go upstream in adversity while maintaining his courage, determination and willpower for constant struggles.

At the very beginning, I had nothing but my dreams and passion. However, if I failed to go on with clenched teeth but retreated due to the difficulties, where could Ibe now?

Xuan Zang, the great Tang Monk, had experienced untold hardships before he returned from the West with true scriptures. For young people who intend to harvest the success of entrepreneurship, they must be down-to-earth, fight endlessly and keep on going despite meeting frustration.

The era calls for young people to move on boldly and go for business. The dream of the great rejuvenation of the Chinese nation needs them to shed sweat on the stage of "hard work" and make a career.

With towering youth inside, we should be brave to fight and to show our true prowess. With a vast space for development, we must carry on the great mission of the era and be prepared to start our own business within the allowable and operable scope. Let us bravely embrace entrepreneurship and taste its ups and downs worthy of the new era.

Part II

Values & Wealth: from Creating to Sharing Wealth

“ **It fills one to give others more than to take from them.**

Lao Tzu, Chapter 81, Tzu (Spring and Autumn Period). ”

We should have the mind of "wishing to get enough houses so that the many poor of the world could be happily sheltered"; cultivate ourselves the belief of "not imposing on others what one does not desire," and all the more have the vision of "keeping the public interests in mind and seeking an everlasting fame."

This is an era of achieving others and ourselves. The era of individual heroism has been past for long, and individual success is far from that of a group. Individual wealth is something so small in comparison with the common prosperity.

04 Good Earner & Good Spender

The value of life can be reflected in two aspects: How to earn and how to spend money. The ability to make money is a manifestation of your ability when you have your personal destiny merged into the times and forge boldly forward with your aspiration in mind. Spending money is an embodiment of your taste. How to spend money and how to make good use of wealth shows your responsibility.

Today, when we say making and spending money, it is not just the number in and out of the accounts. Young people should have the sense of interest and righteousness, and be responsible for their money.

Overnight Upstart &Wealth Creator

Compared with what it was 40 years ago, our entrepreneurial environment has undergone earth-shaking changes, and more and more people are eager to get rich overnight.

However, the real world of wealth and of business have their own rules. We can believe that we may be lucky enough to be the upstarts, but more importantly, our understanding of entrepreneurship must not be just limited to that.

For the difficult Entrepreneurship, everyone has his own path and mode. When you regard overnight wealth as your pursuit, your view of life will be greatly narrowed. When you see wealth creating as a responsibility, your vision will be broadened a lot.

As an entrepreneur, be a wealth creator rather than an upstart. Such a creator, by merging his personal destiny into the times, strives to create more material wealth as well as spiritual wealth.

Starting while in debt, I spent 12 years to make the company a little accomplishment today. From aquaculture industry and digital industry to the media industry, while enabling my partners to get rich, I donated to Sichuan University, Southwest Jiaotong University to the best of my ability, and by various means helped Sichuan's Tibetan areas and Yi areas shackle off poverty. Today, although I enjoy a financial freedom, I am still my old self. Some people doubt this, some ridicule me, and some even feel puzzled. When all these are your choices and views of wealth, how can your vision be limited only to this?

Creating wealth is not just adding a few more zeros to the number in your personal account, much less being addicted to the world of material desires. It is, in its true sense, integrating your personal destiny with the times, bearing in mind your original aspiration, and moving boldly forward.

I often ask myself, "What is your goal? What kind of person do you want to be?What kind of responsibility should you shoulder as one of the young people?"

The road of life is long, so I will search high and low for it. The same is true for entrepreneurship. There is no end to career development. When wealth comes quickly to your way, can you still remain your aspiration?

Many entrepreneurs, regardless of their achievements, remain hardworking. For most of them, the entrepreneurial road is not an easy one, and becomes worse when under the pressure of debt. We ate noodles cooked in plain water with "Laoganma", slept in the bank outlets, and worked all the way for a spacious and bright office area. It is precisely because I have experienced hardships that I understand that nothing is easy to acquire and I am more aware of the significance of creating wealth.

When you have experienced the days of terrible poverty, creating wealth will become your driving force for changing your life. The past has become history but should never be forgotten. Here is a self-evident truth: When one is in possession of wealth, his habit of squandering may destroy decades of efforts overnight.

This is true for both the family and the country. With my own aspiration in mind, I can march on more boldly. Just because the Chinese nation have experienced humiliation in the modern times, we know very well that a country can avoid being bullied only after it becomes strong enough. Just because the Chinese youth keep in mind that part of history, they could live up to their prime time and shoulder their mission bestowed by the era. Just because I have experienced the hardships since I started up my business, I keep warning myself against forgetting the past. This is not only the responsibility for myself, but also for the company and the country.

The road of life is long. While marching forward, we must by no means forget the reason we traveled on. One day, when we are far ahead and get the glorious future, we should be more clear-headed about why we started. As contemporary youths, we must cherish everything we have today, reminding ourselves from time to time of our original aspiration. This is the view of value that in accordance with the spirit of the times, with China's national conditions, and the spiritual pursuit of every communist.

No contemporary youth should limit his vision to material pursuit. In the era of entrepreneurship, we must continue to carry forward the fine tradition of hard work and spend every cent as it is worth. There is no great difference between living in a rented room of 43 square meters and a villa tenfold larger.

The times have given many missions to the youth. The past has become history. Of the vast land, the young people will be the masters. Follow the times and let the world hear the voice of China and admire its contemporary youth. Only by sticking to our original aspiration on the road of wealth creating, can we make a difference and the country develop steadily.

Creating wealth means actively assuming social responsibilities and sacrificing self-achievement. According to Buddhism, life contains three realms ego, great self, and no self. We are all cultivating ourselves, sacrificing the ego, achieving the big self, and finally reaching the realm of no self. By no self, it means no pessimism and inaction, but dedication to the era, the country and the nation.

Sacrificing ego helps achieve the great self. I believe that every young starter of business is eager to be an entrepreneur, a person who is meaningful to society and one with a noble mission. When young people shoulder their responsibilities, the state will have strength, and the nation be full of hope. What we youth bear is the hope of the Party, the country, the people, and the future of the Chinese nation. Only when we establish correct values can we shoulder the mission of the era.

With a small achievement, you go buy a luxury car and a luxury house, then the staff will follow suit. When everyone starts to enjoy himself, the cohesiveness of the company and the magic weapon of entrepreneurship will disappear. What about the plan of our dream for the next ten or even twenty years? At an important moment, the company head should sacrifice his ego self for the great self. He should be clear that wealth creating is the power of the spirit to lead more people to work and create together, instead of indulging himself in money making and material desires, squandering and making no progress.

Less Material Desire & Constant Practice

"This is the best time and this is the worst time." This is an age of extremely rich materials, and also an age of materialism and consumerism. Once you turn on your phone and computer, or walk on the road, all sorts of information that leaps up keeps reminding you -- buy, buy and buy! Consumption tops all!

Will you choose to control, or to be controlled by material desires as a perfect slave? Henry David Thoreau offered his answer in spring more than a hundred years ago.

Tired of the bustling urban life, he built a log cabin near the quiet Lake Walden in his hometown Concord. Within his two-year stay there, he worked, read, pondered, and interacted with various animals and people, felt the nature, and enjoyed a simple "real life".

At the end of the book Walden, Thoreau expressed his ideal life, "Just give me truth instead of love, money, or fame! The life in a human body is like the water in motion, but some novel things keep pouring into the world, while we just endure these incredible stupidities." One of the "stupidities" he mentioned is "most luxury goods and so-called comforts of life."

At that time, the United States was in the period of rapid development from the agricultural to the industrial society. Thoreau was nonplussed by the social environment of impetuosity and enjoyment.

How interesting history is! Today, more than 100 years later, the material wealth of society is unprecedentedly rich, and the same social scene shows up again on this side of the ocean. Now, China has replaced its neighbor Japan as the world's largest consumer of luxury goods.

According to Goldman Sachs' forecast, by 2025, China will take over 44% of the world's luxury market share, the number of luxury consumers will increase to 250 million, and per capita consumption will reach $1,715.

The expansion of consumer market of the luxury not only refelcts the fast development of China's economy and the rapid increase of the number of the rich, but also shows the irrational consumption view many people have. I am not saying that buying luxury goods is a wrong behavior. After all, how to consume is a personal matter. What I mean is the social crisis hidden behind this phenomenon -- people are gradually being manipulated by material desires and become materialistic and even alienated.

Are you really happy and contented when you are busy satisfying yourselves with one material desire after another? Laozi said, “All were simple as they began and then complicated as the result of evolution.” In fact, a person do not need many things for maintaining a basic life. However, in real life, many people are used to paying for their never-ending vanity and desire. The more expensive, the more they buy. This is unnecessary.

However delicately you eat, there are only three meals a day. However spacious and luxurious your house is, you need only one bed at night. You may have many high-end customized suits, but you can only wear one at a time. Your car may be so expensive and cool, but it is only a means of transportation. Is there a basic difference between a bowl of glutinous dumplings and a bowl of porridge at the roadside, and a meal of delicacies in a high-end restaurant?

Yuan Longping, father of hybrid rice, has fed 22% of the population in the world with only 7% of the cultivated land. Nowadays, his super rice is being grown in many places worldwide. As early as 1999, a professional firm assessed that the market value of “Yuan Longping” brand was ¥ 100,89 billion. As for this statement, he admitted that he earns about ¥ 300,000 a year. “I feel contented... Measuring the value of a scientist by wealth is too low-level and too vulgar.”

In the eyes of such a veteran scientist who has solved the problem of feeding Chinese and even the world, money has never been a yardstick for measuring a person’s value. It must be used at the right place and in a meaningful way.

In his daily life, Yuan is extremely frugal and never seek for material enjoyment. In 2001, when attending the Honorary Doctoral Ceremony of the Chinese University of Hong Kong, he wore a tie for only ¥ 10 or more.

Wearing plain clothes, taking economy-class flight, and owning a domestically produced scooter worth ¥100,000, Yuan also turned his luxury house provided by the state into a scientific research center, and used various bonuses to set up Yuan Longping Technology Award Fund... A reporter asked him why he didn't buy a big house. He replied, "A big but unoc-cupied house is empty and has no use."

With his lifetime of plain clothing and usual stay in the rice fields, this very aged scientist has told everyone with his actions, "No need to think highly of fame and fortune, nor material requirements."

In real life, many people are so enslaved by endless material desires that they spend money in an unrestrained and thoughtless way, and some even do so beyond their own affordability. This is actually a kind of sorrow. People should be able to control things, but not be controlled by things of their own creation.

Excessive material desires will swallow up your life, make your life infinitely complicated, and exhaust you by sending around material pursuit all day. In this way, one has no energy or time for the higher-level spiritual life. Some people think that the - label on products can show their extraordinary taste. In fact, it is never material, but spirit, that determines who you are. To a certain extent, material desires are preventing you from becoming a better self.

How to escape the control of material desires? There is no other way but simplifying life and practicing it constantly.

In terms of material desire, we should try to be as simple as possible. Thoreau described that, "Plunge yourself deep into life, suck up the marrow of life, live it fully but simply, remove all that is not part of life, and keep it at bay in the most basic form. Simple, simple, and simple."

Reducing material desires is a long practice yet many a hindrance. On the way, you may face various temptations, be ridiculed by others, or be knocked down by sudden vanity and a possessive desire. However, as long as you persist, you will certainly gain something, like a noble and simple state of life, a quiet and peaceful mood, or true happiness from the bottom of your heart.

I have a deep understanding of this. In life, I try to simplify my material need as much as possible. I do not smoke, drink, visit nightclubs, or care about eating and drinking. Going out to work, I hail a taxi. On a business trip, I take economy class. As an entrepreneur and dreamer, it is normal to pour all of your love in your business. To this end, you will willingly simplify your life and invest all your wealth, energy and even time to it. Under the guidance of your dream, you will feel happy and satisfied every day.

Simplifying material needs is a virtue for the individual, a fashion for the society and a spirit for the country and the nation. Just imagine what a terrible thing it would be if most people of a country and nation were addicted to material enjoyment!

Today, China's GDP has ranked second in the world, yet it is still far from being developed, with many people failing to live a rich life. In order to build a fair and affluent country, as the new generation burdened with responsibilities, we need to continuously carry on this arduous and simple style, to light up our youth through struggle and hard work, and to create more values for the society.

Wealth Control & Individual Success

Over the past 40 years of reform and opening up, China has undergone tremendous changes, and its economic growth has grown rapidly. The trend has been rapid, and Huawei, Gree, high-speed rail, and shared bicycle have been born... What is Made in China has gone global; China's Internet is has been leading the world; and some well-known major enterprises have been leading the development of China's economy.

Behind these enterprises is the great surge of wealth and the rise of countless entrepreneurs. Today, under the new normal of economic development, promoting entrepreneurship and establishing a correct view of wealth have been placed in a more important position.

Today, with the rapid development of economy, the way you control your wealth directly determines your life direction. In other words, your view of wealth directly influences your achievements in life.

Wealth may mean money only to many people. If we think in another way, it actually, consists of material wealth and spiritual wealth. Everyone must live, so material wealth is indeed important, but the effect of spiritual wealth should never be ignored.

The 12-year entrepreneurial experience tells me that people must not just live in the material world, but more live in the spiritual world.

Everyone has their own vision and responsibility, and most ordinary people are far less rich than entrepreneurs are. On the great stage of China or even the world, generations of entrepreneurs have been in step with the times and chosen to contribute their own energy to the society. Imagine, how will you manipulate your wealth if you achieve financial freedom?

Frankly speaking, what an entrepreneur has earned is not his. It belongs to the society and the state, to the public, and he is just its keeper. How to spend money, how to better control wealth and do more meaningful things, these are what we need to think about.

One of the older generation of entrepreneurs Cao Dewang once said, "I am one of the first-generation beneficiaries from the reform and opening up. The money I have earned must be returned to society." That era has offered such good environments and policies that a group of reform practitioners and beneficiaries has emerged. In the new era, while creating wealth, young entrepreneurs should cultivate a correct view of wealth and never forget to assume our social responsibilities.

Compared with businessmen and merchants, entrepreneurs are more respectable. They have propelled the development of enterprises in the tide of reform and opening up and played an invaluable role in freeing China from lagging behind to following others and then to surpassing them. True entrepreneurs think that the interests of the country and the society are above all else. They have made important contributions to the creation of jobs for the society and economic development.

The achievement and success in your career and life are not determined by how much you have gained, but by how much you have contributed to the country. After earning money, how to feed back the society is the concept of wealth that the younger generation of entrepreneurs should have.

There are countless beneficiaries of the times, and we are all part of them. As members of the younger generation who have grown up in a socialist country, many poor students like me who could walk out of a mountain village and own today's achievements and wealth owe a lot to the opportunities given by the state and society.

As a young man and entrepreneur, I consider myself duty-bound to the country and to the building of a well-off society in an all-round way. Cao Dewang said, "China's hope lies in the consciousness of its own people. If there is one in every industry who persistently links his undertaking to his country, he can not only serve as a leader in his own industry, creating wealth for himself and the society, but has the opportunity to be on a greater stage in the world, creating more values and wealth."

Money is a manifestation of the value of life, but we must not be enslaved by it.The value orientation of the youth plays a vital role in the value orientation of the society.

Within the environments of the state and its policies, making money for the accumulation of wealth is a manifestation of personal ability and talents. However, the ever-increasing amount of money means the growing responsibility as well. China is now in a critical period of economic transformation, so entrepreneurs must more bravely shoulder their mission and be responsible for the society.

An entrepreneur should bear a little more pressure and do his best for the society. If one follows material wealth blindly, thinking it the only measure of life, he will eventually lose himself.

Money is taken from and should be given back to the people. The country and the era have given you the opportunity to become a billionaire and accumulate huge amounts of property. In the same way, you should give some feedback to this era and contribute to the sustainable and healthy development of the economy of the society.

Perhaps, your company is not strong enough at present, because investment accounts for many financial expenses on top of risk and public welfare expenditures. Yet, as wealth changes, corporate spending will change. The main spending always lies in two parts: investment and public welfare, which is what I, as an entrepreneur, will be doing in the few decades.

Each of us must set up a correct view of wealth and consciously become the master of money.

How does Bill Gates, the world's richest man, view money? He does not have a private driver or a private jet, but travels in first class on any official business trips. He never wears clothes with famous brands or spends more than necessary on parking.

He is not one who works for money. Entrepreneurship is just his life experience, and wealth is just a yardstick for quantifying his value. He once went with a friend to the Hilton Hotel for a meeting. They were a few minutes late and there was no parking space left. The friend proposed to park in the place for the Hotel's VIPs, but Gates disagreed. The friend said, "It's on me." Gates still refused. The reason is very simple. It needed an extra $12 for parking, which he thought not worth it.

The increase in wealth did not change his life. He said, "I am only the keeper of this wealth, which is to be used in the most suitable way." With a huge amount of wealth, Gates has become neither a stubborn miser nor a spendthrift. He is the master of money.

The value of life lies in how to make and how to spend money. The era has created a lot of opportunities for us youth in such an advantageous environment. Our dream pattern has been given higher expectations and more epochal significance. When we fight and create material wealth, we must know how to control and pay it back to the society.

The youth and young entrepreneurs should correct their views on wealth, raise their own sails of life in the struggle, be dream-chasers with ideals, pursuits and commitments, do something in this era, and represent China's appearance in the world.

Spiritual Wealth & Material Wealth

Between material wealth and spiritual wealth, which matters more? How to understand the relationship between the two?

Some people bias toward the latter. Being caught in poverty all their life, they are full of happiness. Some people value material wealth and feel that a luxury car and a gold necklace are the greatest enjoyment and fun in human life.

Lev Tolstoy once said, "Lack of money is a sad thing, but excessive possession of it is something worse." It must be a painful experience without money, but too much of it cannot be necessarily good. Material wealth and spiritual wealth never work against but reinforce each other in a harmonious way.

If I have to choose, I will do the latter without the least hesitation.

For an individual, however much material wealth he owns, his life will be a shallow one if his spiritual world is empty.

Material wealth makes one to achieve or lose freedom. Similarly, material wealth can increase or decrease his spiritual wealth.

Just imagine what would befall a person devoid of spiritual wealth despite his great material wealth. For the good part, he may stop forging ahead and rest on his laurels. For the bad part, he may squander the last bit of family property and even harm the society.

Unless with the prerequisite of rich spiritual wealth, too much material wealth will probably ruin its owner.

In the autobiography of the famous British comedian Charlie Chaplin, there is such a short story: Chaplin was so ecstatic when he received the first huge amount of money. At that moment, a producer warned him not to be stuck in the greed for money. Chaplin was puzzled and asked him the reason. The producer said, "When you can rationally control the money in your hands, you will be able to get psychological freedom. But if you don't know how to spend it, you will be in a stone's throw from your ruin." This plunged Chaplin into deep thinking. Later, he grew up as a film master of his time and had never been lured by the market and money, which, to a certain extent, was quite related to his rational and healthy concept of money.

Ancient Chinese historian Sima Qian once said, "The world is full of people going after profits here, there and everywhere." Everyone is working hard for wealth, which is understandable, because without material or money, none can survive. However, there is no end to the sea of wealth. It is important to earn money, but how to use material wealth will be quite a test for people.

It is undeniable that such a phenomenon exists: many wealthy people buy sports cars, luxury houses, yachts and private jets. On their wedding nights, they can have the whole Maldives, and even give people Porsche and ship on "live"…

How to spend money is a private matter, but the impact of such showy behavior on society cannot be ignored. When the bad habits of showing off wealth or hatred of the rich spread afar, what impact will it have on the growth of the next generation?

It is a fact that ordinary and rich people have their own Lifestyles. In addition to the increase in spiritual wealth based on material wealth, the rich should think more about how to do good things for the whole society as well.

Confucius said, "Only when the poor gets rich will they know shame and learn etiquettes." Unless a person solves his problem of three meals a day, he can hardly accept the most basic education, let alone to create more wealth for himself or others. However, if a person with a lot of money cares only for material enjoyment without the least awareness of promoting his spiritual realm to benefit the society, he is more pitiable than the former who is left no other choice.

Material wealth perishes easily, but spiritual wealth lasts forever. The former is something fluid and cannot perpetuate, while spiritual wealth can go down to future generations and shine through the ages.

"Empty is the mansion once visited in a row; a dancing hall is under the grass that lies low; all carved beams are in spider thread; green yarn is stuck on the windows instead..." In *The Dream of Red Mansions*, Cao Xueqin wrote this down to describe the ups and downs of Jia, Shi and Wang families.

We often say that richness can hardly outlast three generations. It is reasonable. If the descendants, forgetting the teachings of their ancestors, become arrogant and wallow in extravagance, they will eventually go to the dogs. Numerous facts have proved that, without any thought of progress or spiritual wealth for support, gold and silver, however much, will be gone sooner or later.

Therefore, what is spiritual wealth? It covers too wide a range to be introduced precisely. Spiritual quality, dream, knowledge and thinking are all parts of it.

Only after spiritual wealth is enriched can material wealth be the same. Because the former is the driving force that guides people to create more material wealth.

Spiritual wealth seems invisible, but once the opportunity shows up, it can create much material wealth for both individuals and the society. In the era full of challenges and opportunities, an idea or a quote can be transformed into material wealth. However, if you are thinking of how to get rich and profits, success will hardly viist you. For an entrepreneur who is spiritually rich and dares to fight hard, material wealth will patronize him sooner or later.

I have always been thinking about why I can go so far. In fact, it is not difficult to answer. In the past few years, each of my experiences has been like a sharp blade, cutting my skin and encrusting the wound. The spiritual wealth has never left me when I was learning, starting up business, dreaming and doing other things. Only with spiritual enrichment, can I practice my entrepreneurial dream without hesitation and fear.

Whether poor or rich, you can never afford the loss of your spiritual wealth. If the accumulation of material wealth is based on spiritual wealth, then the growth of spiritual wealth will become an inexhaustible source for material wealth. In other words, the lack of spiritual wealth will certainly lead to the shortage of material wealth.

Spiritual wealth sometimes plays a decisive role in the creation and regeneration of material wealth for an individual, an enterprise and the state. In contemporary China, with the calls of the spiritual wealth such as the core socialist values and the Chinese Dream, if we dare to think and dare to do, and strive for the prosperity of our nation, we can create immeasurable material wealth for the country and the world.

Entrepreneurship & Wealth Creation

Everyone wants to do something, start his own business, and create wealth. How many steps does one need to take from nearly nothing to almost everything? No one can be sure of that.

In the great river of entrepreneurship, countless people have stepped in and out. In the end, some people have accomplished nothing while others have achieved both fame and fortune. This kind of stories are innumerable. Some say that poverty makes people loners, while wealth makes them the revelers. This very road from entrepreneurship to wealth creation is not just that simple.

How to truly create wealth? First, we must understand what entrepreneurship and wealth creating mean.

The former is a springboard for wealth creation, which contains enterprise management. It is also the embodiment of dreams and courage. Creating wealth is creating value. For enterprises, wealth is not just about making profits for the enterprise, but also creating values for the society. The core of the heritage of enterprise is to transmit its value to make it develop sustainably on the one hand, and shoulder its social responsibility on the other.

Entrepreneurship itself is a process of elimination. To sustain a long-term development, an enterprise must be closely linked to the destiny of the country.

The establishment of the economic system for the socialist market has inspired entrepreneurs' unlimited vitality. The courageous and sharp-minded ones have pushed the Chinese economy forward from its backwardness, to the state of following others, and finally to the state of surpassing them. It must be admitted that the country and the era have given them opportunities for development. In return, the enterprises have promoted the continuous development of the national economy.

In any era, only when the country has created a stable environment for development, can the individuals have the opportunity to show their value. I was born in the countryside. It was the national education policy that brought me out of the mountain village. It was the China's entrepreneurial policies that helped me get on the road to entrepreneurship. What are the correct views on wealth creation? Understanding the love for the Party and the country is one of the most important views on wealth creation.

However rich individuals and enterprises are, we will still be attacked and bullied if the country is not strong enough. For China to get strong, the younger generation must spend all their life on wealth creation, and entrepreneurs must assume the mission of the age.

A truly great enterprise, or a truly responsible entrepreneur, cannot just keep his eyes and aspiration on capital accumulation and neglect his social responsibility. As I think of the past 12-year struggle, I have got to know that I can go so far because I have cherished my dream, have experienced many times working for "five plus two, namely, a week " and "white plus black, namely, day and night". That is how my company has developed from few staffers to about one thousand employees, who have been of one mind and worked for one dream.

Nothing is easy to come by on earth. Along the way, we have received countless support and encouragement, which have made us more grateful and more willing to contribute to society as much as we can. Within the company, we have formed a team of volunteers to provide services to the community and bring our kindness to stay-at-home children free of charge.

From entrepreneurship to wealth creation, it is necessary to guard against arrogance, impetuosity and opportunism. This is not only beneficial for people to pursue the truth and scale the peak, but also to cultivate their entrepreneurial spirit. In my company, the younger generation is the dominant force. I attach importance to the cultivation of their correct values and let them develop the good habits of being down-to-earth and pragmatic.

None of the countless successful people has failed to be down-to-earth with a footprint in each step. On Mt. Ailao, Chu Shijian started from scratch and explored and gradually mastered all techniques concerning orange planting, eventually becoming king of oranges. Zong Qinghou had started by selling soda water from one street or lane to another on his tricycle before he formed Wahaha Group. You have to believe that you will never be deceived by your own work, and it will never be wrong of you to be down-to-earth.

Today, when the economy is developing at a high speed, and the industry faces one opportunity or challenge after another. No enterprise is to walk away from the rules but obey the law and assume social responsibility instead while riding bravely on the wind. Remaining modest so as not to hit the rocks is the important criterion for the survival and development of an enterprise.

The business leader is the chief and more the spiritual leader. With thousands of employees working and struggling with you, your positive role as the spiritual leader should be properly played, because every move of yours can touch each and every one from the top down. Your example with high standards can quietly and subtly influence and change those around or under you, so that a vigorous and progressive atmosphere can be formed among the young people. As time goes on, such a spiritual style will be part of the company's wealth as well as its core competitiveness.

What do top companies rely on? Culture or corporate spirit. If an enterprise leader has lost the thought of struggle, what does he turn to for business? Although you keep shouting slogans without struggling for your business, how can you lead your company? You have to lead your employees to establish the correct view of values and struggle so that they may have a higher pursuit and higher value orientation.

As companies grow bigger, wealth increases. But can you say that you are near wealth creation with more and more money in your possession? This understanding is too one-sided. The true wealth creation has its feature of the era. It is an effort of keeping at heart your aspiration, a responsibility to the world, and the lead and dissemination of spiritual power.

Talent is the driving force behind the company development, so the role of employees can never be ignored. Respect talents so they can live a dignified life, which has an important role in promoting corporate development. After you have been in business for many years, there are still dozens of veteran employees working hard with you. Let me congratulate you on your possession of the greatest wealth.

Only with the excellent quality of hard work and self-reliance can we promote the growth of the company and realize personal values. We all know that entrepreneurship is difficult, but hasn't Huawei done like this in the past? None can achieve excellence hands down. Without making great efforts and experiencing something extraordinary in the ordinary world, how can you take the lead?

An enterprise creates wealth not just for its own. A truly great one won't keep its vision and ambition to money only, but to the social responsibility for the country.

In the past 40 years, the Chinese economy has developed from a disorderly barbaric growth to a state of order, innovation and sharing. This achievement is certainly gratifying. However, in the aspect of social development, we still face many challenges, for example, the uneven distribution of wealth, middle-income trap, lack of sustainable development, serious environmental pollution, and so on. To solve these problems, the time calls for companies to re-examine their social roles and responsibilities.

In the future, the Chinese Dream will be passed down from generation to generation. As young entrepreneurs, we must realize the dream of a strong country and propel the great rejuvenation of the Chinese nation by creating values, assuming social responsibilities, and opening up new horizons for the future of the motherland.

As young people of the new era, we must bear in mind our mission, original aspiration and, with the spirit of self-reliance, the quality of optimism and generosity, and the style of down-to-earth effort, solve more employment problems in the process of enterprise development, shoulder more social responsibilities, and actively repay the society and the era with gratitude.

In such a great era, with the power of dream behind us and with the state as our sol id backing, we youth should always rush on and take the lead.

05 Wealth for One & Wealth for All

From the founding of New China in 1949 to the present, generations of Party leaders have been working tirelessly to achieve common prosperity and lead the people to pursue a better life. Richness for one person is a small case while that for a group is common prosperity. Today, the contradiction between the people's growing need for a better life and inadequate and unbalanced development has become the major one in Chinese society. We younger generation should do our best all the time so as to contribute to the realization of common prosperity.

Success by One & Success by a Group

Jack Welch, former president of General Electric, said, "For my success, 10% is based on my personal and enterprising spirit, and 90% on the strong team that leans on me."The power of a person is limited, not to mention the present era of knowledge explosion today. Only by uniting more people to work together can you get a feel of the times.

Teamwork can lead to a greater chance for success. We are in an era of ever-changing time. Every minute or second may witness it. In today's increasingly fierce competition, nothing in the world can be done singly because the era of "Lone Ranger" has gone forever.

An individual, no matter how powerful and talented, has but limited ability, but a system is another matter because of its broader vision. If you choose to go alone, the road ahead will narrow down, and those who choose like-minded people will struggle to get closer and closer to success.

With teamwork, even ants can beat a lion. "If you see an antelope running on the African savanna, there must be a lion after it; if you see the lion running, there must be an elephant being angered; if you see hundreds of lions and elephants running, there must be an army corps of ants coming. " This is an impressive passage in *Animal World*.

The power generated by teamwork is unimaginable. A small ant can be smashed with one finger, but a group of ants united as one can scatter lions and elephants. Hence the power of a team.

We cannot guarantee that an individual can do everything, but we can build a system to accomplish things that no individual can by means of its power to get individuals together.

In the past seven years, I have been leading the staff from debt to zero, then to one, then to one hundred. Our noodles cooked in plain water together with the sauce called "laoganma" has given birth to today's Nanjiao Media. But for our passion and teamwork, we could hardly last till now.

"One man doesn't make an array. One wood doesn't make a forest." A streamlet has to flow into the sea before it looks magnificent. No matter how hard one works, he is nothing against the power of a system.

A person rowing against the current will soon stop owing to its resistance and be washed farther and farther away from his target, but it will be much easier and faster to go upstream if there are trackers from the shore.

It doesn't matter who a person is, but what matters is that a group of persons is standing behind him!

You may work hard, but still need a hardworking team to fight with you; you may work hard, but still need to follow a leader to grow quickly.

An enterprise is the main body of social innovation, and an entrepreneur is the soul of enterprise innovation. In a certain sense, the reason why an entrepreneur is made so largely depends on his innovative spirit.

An entrepreneur is a scarce resource and valuable asset to the society. He leads his enterprise to create a large amount of material wealth and spiritual wealth, so he should shoulder the great mission of prospering the economy and bear the responsibility for serving the public. On an analysis of the entrepreneurial process of various entrepreneurs, we have found that they generally have a strong sense of innovation, perseverance, flexible market sense, scientific decision-making ability, and communication skills.

An entrepreneur is of great importance to the dream description and future planning of his company. The father of management Drucker once said, "The first priority for the leader is to define the mission, which is also his original aspiration. While learning and developing leadership, we often need to ask ourselves: What is my original aspiration?"

If a leader is far-sighted, the employees will feel the hope of the company and are willing to make it happen with him. But if the leader is short-sighted and has no clear vision or big dream, he can neither influence those below nor keep the talented people.

A leader must have some glittering qualities at the same time. For example, the spirits of struggle and perseverance, no fear of failure and courage enough to be challenged, the spirit of integrity that adheres to principles and does what is necessary. Without all these, he cannot win respect and trust from employees.

Being a person or doing something, one must seek truth from facts and be responsible, which are what every leader should possess.

Others & Oneself

Over the past 40 years, our life has changed at a speed that is visible to the naked eye: widened houses, taller buildings, more abundant foods on the table, more cars, more beautiful clothes, and more friends.

In the past five years alone, more than 60 million people in China have been steadily lifted out of poverty; the education in the central and western regions has been strengthened; the employment situation has been constantly improving; the income growth rate of urban and rural residents has exceeded the rate of economic development; the middle-income group has been continuously expanding; people's health and medical care have been greatly improved and the social governance system has been more complete...

We are very clear that, behind these ever-changing changes, it is by no means the result of the efforts of a certain person or a group but that of the struggle of a country and a nation.

Today, at the critical moment of reform and opening up, everyone is the center of the times. We are more aware that the future depends on everyone to create, and the future prosperity will belongs to the whole people. Only by helping others to make it can one help himself.

In the case of an enterprise, helping others is to respect and care for employees, protect their rights, and sharpen their competitiveness. As an entrepreneur, you cannot realize your dream unless you provide a platform for others.

Respect and care for others, so that everyone has a sense of acquisition and happiness.

At any stage, people are the key to the progress of the times. A country needs them for development, and a company needs them for wealth creating. Respecting talent and employees means respecting the company itself.

If the employees of a company are mostly from the rural area, they may not own high academic qualifications, their families are not rich, and cannot be compared with others as for various conditions. But in a big city, they also want to find the value of existence and the goal of life. You may find that they are actually the majority of society, just like you. They are so ordinary but also can create values.

Respecting employees is the key to the company development. The relationship between the company and employees is not just about money. If they are close to each other like family members in your company, and each is placed in a fair and open way, the overall atmosphere will be completely new. To be people-oriented is to respect their rights, help them realize their values of life while giving them humanistic care.

If a company is cared about employees in every aspect by providing them with good accommodations such as air conditioners, refrigerators, washing machines, water heaters, WiFi and other living equipment; if it brings even their parents along in an organized travel, do you think it will get a high rate of turnover? As long as this people-oriented culture is rooted in the company, there will be a strong sense of belonging and happiness among the employees.

Zhang Yong, founder of Haidilao, once said that employees should be treated as relatives. Its excellent service to the public is the result of its true respect for employees.

I have made such an arrangement: Visit some excellent staff back home every Spring Festival with a group of employees, holding group banquets, setting off fireworks in their honor, which helps enhance their sense of identity and belonging.

In any era, only by striving for others can you achieve yourself. Respecting and caring for everyone so as to let him live with dignity is the best way to achieve others.

A company's development is preconditioned by the protection of the employees' legitimate rights and interests. Wealth is created by everyone, and protecting individual rights is to consolidate the foundation of the company.

The enterprise is like a machine, and no single part alone can work properly. In the enterprise and the team, it is necessary to clarify that the founder is only a role assigned by the division of labor. I have heard such a sentence: In the future, there are platforms only but no companies, leaders only but no bosses, and partners only but no employees.

Today, when we emphasize the protection of employees' rights and interests, it must not be a lip service, but a practical action. This is an era in which everyone is closely connected. Everyone has the right to have a good life and to pursue happiness. Creating better conditions for employees is to create a better future for the company.

From the digital to the media era, in the process of corporate transformation, I still have the original employees along. In my most difficult time, it is owing to their readiness for timely help that the company still exists today. When you started a business, few friends and brothers around you had chosen to work hard with you, but a group of strangers choosing to believe in you because of their dreams. Then what reason do you have to not thank them? If you don't even care for those who have been following you, what's the use talking about gratitude, let alone the realization of the value of life?

Should my company have the chance to go public one day, its funds for pensions and next-generation education will be substantially increased. I will set up my own education group. From kindergarten to university, the children of the employees can attend each directly. It is even possible that the children of excellent employees will do so entirely at the cost of the company.

In addition, few employees' parents enjoy social security and pensions, and can hardly bear the cost of a major illness. The company will set up pension funds, crowd-funding plans and so on for relieving them of such worries.

This is the era for creating and sharing wealth, and also the era for helping others and yourself. Only by safeguarding the rights and interests of employees and reducing their worries can we promote the enterprise development more effectively. An enterprise is an important force in the development of the country. When it is well managed, the social and economic level can rise steadily across the country.

Only by enhancing the core competitiveness of employees can the enterprise go farther.

Talented people make the core competitiveness of an enterprise, so, for a company to go farther, enhancing the power of employees is a must. In the past, present and future, all competition is the competition of talent.

Those who work hard for the company should be given something in return. In the future, my company will launch a training program to send plenty of outstanding employees abroad, so that they can learn management and operation and return in half a year. It can even implement an early retirement plan and allocate specific funds for retirement. If an employee does not want to retire, the company provides training, re-employment and entrepreneurship. It can also set up investment funds. If employees are willing to invest, it will help them manage their finance. This is an era of wealth creation for all when one gains while he gives and grows while he pays.

The rise and fall of an enterprise concerns all the employees. For an entrepreneur, the ideal entrepreneurship may be that when the company is in difficulty one day, its employees still choose to work with its leader to tide over the storm.Undoubtedly, employees, while realizing their life values at work, their continuous creativity will grow stronger, and the company will last longer. The development of an enterprise raises the overall economic strength of the country, which helps to achieve not only the national cause, but also the enterprise itself, and every employee of the enterprise.

Material & Spiritual Prosperity

What is the biggest difference between ordinary and great companies?

An ordinary enterprise exists for shareholders and employees, its main purpose being to create material wealth. A great one exists for the society, the country, and even all human beings. They create a large amount of spiritual and cultural wealth in addition to huge material wealth. In terms of competitiveness and social contributions, the latter is far stronger than the former, and its value of existence and pattern is beyond the reach of the former.

Georg Wilhelm Friedrich Hegel once said, "The ideal figure must be reflected on his satisfaction not only with material needs, but also with spiritual interests." Material and spiritual needs achieve mutual prosperity, and an ideal figure needs to do this, so does a great company with ideals.

A great and respectable enterprise should internally create a large amount of material wealth and spiritual wealth, fully satisfying the dual needs of employees at either level, and externally create a lot of both in a steady way for the country, society and all mankind.

Since the reform and opening up, the trend of entrepreneurship has swept across the country. In each wave, a group of starters have ventured into the sea of business and birthed many excellent enterprises. Huawei is one of the best.

Huawei pays heed not only to its employees' material benefits, but also to their spiritual needs. In a letter to Huawei's new employees, Ren wrote, "Huawei's common value system is to establish a corporate culture that contributes to the world, to society, and to the motherland. This culture, open and inclusive, is a constant absorption of the excellent culture and management in the world... Material resources will eventually be exhausted, but culture won't. A high-tech enterprise can't go without its culture, which alone can support its sustainable development, and Huawei's culture is the culture of hard struggle. All its connotations come from the advanced and reasonable parts of the world, from all nationalities, partners, even from counterparts..."

Internally, Huawei is committed to achieving the mutual wealth of employees at the material and spiritual levels. Externally, Huawei, though located in China, is a company with the whole world in mind. Since its establishment, it has been continuously creating new technological products and putting forward its corporate culture as contributions to the country and the world.

Material wealth, as the most basic thing for the survival and development of an enterprise, is an indispensable part of it. After solving that, the enterprise must find ways to propel its creation and accumulation of material wealth for better development.

If we say that material wealth, as the hard power, is the strong backing of an enterprise, then, spiritual wealth, as the soft power, is the source of power to support it and its employees. Spiritual wealth is indispensable to the company development from start to finish, unlike the step-by-step accumulation of material wealth. Therefore, it is unscientific to hold the idea of the more developed a company, the better its corporate culture.

The spiritual wealth of an enterprise cannot be measured and analyzed simply with its amount and depth. It can only be said that at every stage of enterprise development, its spiritual culture has a different expression with its own focus.

Sometimes, I cannot help thinking of the days when we were full of dare and daring at work. At that time, struggling days and nights for weeks, I used to go home by the last metro. When in a tight spot, we had noodles with "laoganma" for days. Sometimes we failed to get our wages. When the dormitory had no beds to spare, some veteran employees simply went for the night in the room for a bank ATM lay. At 7 or 8 o'clock in the morning, they returned for some washing and went straight to work at the Digital Square. We started from a shop of more than 50 square meters with four simple desks only.

Without this spirit of struggle and hard work, Lanjiao Media would be found nowhere today. This spiritual wealth, even if reviewed at this moment, is commendable. However, the accumulation of its spiritual wealth is not a process from less to more, because from the moment of its establishment our spiritual wealth was strong enough.

Now, Lanjiao Media has already had certain strength, successfully passed its initial stage of survival, and smoothly entered the next stage of development. At this crossroads, I urge myself to achieve the common prosperity of the material and spiritual needs for all employees: First, share part of the material wealth accumulated with the employees as a return. Secondly, continue to be a good example, pay more attention to its teamwork building, summarize and refine its spiritual and cultural connotations to meet the growing cultural needs of employees.

The report to the 19th National CPC Congress pointed out, "It is necessary to create more material wealth and spiritual wealth to meet the people's growing needs for a better life, and to provide more high-quality ecological products to meet the growing ecological needs of the people."

The great era calls for more great enterprises. Both the enterprise and the entre preneur of the new era should have the responsibility and obligation to practice the above requirements, starting from within the enterprise and gradually spreading to the local area, to the nation and to the world, enabling more people to realize both material wealth and spiritual wealth.

All for One & One for All

There is a Chinese company that has neither gone public nor accepted any third-party investment, but the founder holds less than 1% of the shares. Where have the others gone? The answer is: In the hands of the Employees Stock Holding Committee acting on their behalf. Should an employee leave his post, his share will be given back in cash immediately by the company, even if it is worth tens of millions of dollars.

This company is called Huawei, and such a system is decided by his leader Ren himself. He once said, "I had designed the employee stock ownership system when I started the company. Through benefit sharing, I united the employees as one. At that time, I didn't quite understand the option system, much less that the West is very developed in this respect with various incentives. Based on my own past setbacks, I realized that I should share responsibility and benefits with my employees. At the beginning of the establishment, I discussed this practice with my father and got his strong support. He was a major of Economics in the 1930s. This unintended flower is now blooming so brilliantly and has also made Huawei such a success."

The design of Huawei's joint-stock system for all is unique in the world. When Sam Walton's "everyone is a shareholder" was designed for Wal-Mart, it did not do so well, nor did the management philosophy of "Respect Heaven and Love People" advocated by Inamori Kazuo. Ren Zhengfei's high vision and great wisdom are convincing.

It is because he can stand at the height of "one for all" that he has got the happiness of "all for one." The achievements of Huawei over the past 30 years are the best proof.

Today, "one for all, all for one" is a view of era-sharing values. In this era when everyone is closely connected, human distance is infinitely narrowed, so is their relationship close.

In life, every time after we use the taxi software, the driver will ask amicably whether we can give him a five-star rating. This click will increase his credibility, and this means that he will receive more orders and earn more money. A praise from the passenger's use of a thumb at this time does not cost money but can create more wealth for the driver. That is to say, any of our small action may have an impact on others. Under the influence of the Internet, the relationship between people has become closer, and it is easier to establish connections.

As early as 1967, the American social psychologist Milgram put forward the famous "six-degree division theory". He said, "The distance between you and any stranger will not exceed five persons, that is, you can know any stranger through five more persons." According to this theory, there are only five people between you and any stranger in the world, regardless of the stranger's country, race and color.

In 2001, a research team at Columbia University Sociology Department conducted an experiment on the Internet. They set up an experimental website with 18 people in different countries. Afterwards, volunteers sent emails to friends and relatives who are most likely to achieve the task. As a result, 384 emails arrived at the destination, and on average, it took only five to seven steps to pass it onto the target.

In the future, the distance between people will be even shorter, so is the gap between two strangers. Sharing is always mutual and indispensable to each and every one.

The concept of family and country in China has a long history, and our sense of well-being always carries a group feature. Happiness has a shared meaning within a family, a business and a country. "Before your success, strive for self-cultivation; when in success, try to serve the world." After one individual achieves prosperity, he must not forget to repay the society.

If only "all for one" dominates, it will just put yourself in the center of the world. The French materialist philosopher Diderot used a very interesting phrase, "In a mad moment, the piano with feelings once thought that it was the only one in the world, and all the harmony of the universe happened to it."

If only "one for all" dominates, which is indeed a lofty ideal to be pursued, and even more the main theme of contemporary society, it is not in line with social reality. Only when the two are balanced can they promote each other. Only after all are for one can there be one for all. To realize this shared value, either for a country or for an enterprise, we must unswervingly follow the path of mutual prosperity.

"One for all" is a manifestation of Confucian "not imposing on others what one does not desire." The concept of "one for all" has no boundary, and it can be small or big. For an enterprise, this concept of sharing wealth has three levels: the lowest is to share wealth with the family members; the second is to share wealth with the original team, employees, and partners; and the universally lofty one is to share wealth with society and the times.

Since the company started, I have taken the lead in the establishment of a service team of volunteers for the community and stay-at-home children. These small things have turned into a positive energy.

The "one for all" view of value sharing is by no means just the sharing of material wealth, but also that of spiritual wealth. I once gave a speech at the High School affiliated to Southwest Jiaotong University. What most touched me was a first-year student with leukemia. He said that every time he felt that he couldn't hold on, he would think of me. The boy had quietly taken me as a spiritual role model.

The progress of the times has detailed the social division of labor. The new industry has created more opportunities at the new juncture, and the contemporary youth have a broader stage than ever before. Based on the wealth acquired from the times and the country, we entrepreneurs should give something in return and elevate the view of values "one for all."

As young people of the new era, we shoulder the great mission of the times. Only by working hard and forging ahead to the best of our ability can we be worthy of this era.

As young entrepreneurs, we must assume our social responsibilities. It is clear that individual richness is nothing before common prosperity. While leading corporate employees to create wealth, we must create values for the whole of society.

Only after we young generation have a good understanding of the "all for one, one for all" of personal destiny being closely related to the times and enhance our personal responsibility can we go farther on the road of life.

No enterprise can go without the times it belongs to. Regardless of corporate development or personal growth, we must be grateful for the times and for the environment created by the country. While being rooted in the ordinary world, we must lead the fashion of the times. This is the best interpretation of "all for one, one for all".

06 Repay Society & Realize Chinese Dream

Youth in its prime means the time for struggle. We stand abreast of the times and set sail in the environment provided by the state and society. Meanwhile, we youth should remember them.

For truly great men, look to this age alone! To realizing the Chinese Dream of the great rejuvenation of the Chinese nation, the power of youth is indispensable. Only when those of my generation can work hard for the Chinese Dream and the ideal of human life in the struggle and keep our youthful passion with gratitude can we live up to the good times.

Donate Today & Receive Tomorrow

There are three realms in life: sights of yourself, heaven and earth, and all beings. First of all, people must truly understand themselves and find what their foundation is. Secondly, people must rise from the realm of ego to that of great self, broadening their vision. "A saint follows the will of the people rather than his own." In the end, people will return to the earth, constantly lowering themselves, and fully integrating what they see and feel into those of all beings.

Like human life, doing business can also be divided into three realms. In the "sight of yourself" stage, an enterprise must be self-reliant while striving for survival, and gradually explore its core competitiveness while giving no trouble to society and the country. In the "sight of heaven and earth" stage, it must bravely move toward a broader stage, constantly struggle and strive for the upper reaches. At the same time, it should assume certain social responsibilities. In the "sight of all beings" stage, it must assume more social responsibilities by considering how to give something back to the whole society and the country, and how to grow into a great enterprise so as to benefit the country and the people and even all mankind.

Today, entrepreneurs are one of the wealthiest groups. More gain means greater responsibility as a matter of course. They should assume social responsibilities with the country in mind.

Today, human society has entered an era of extreme material and spiritual enrichment. The times produces its heroes. It is precisely in the international context of peaceful development that many businessmen and entrepreneurs have seized the opportunity after the trend for creating untold myths of wealth and accumulating a large amount of material wealth.

However, a global look reveals that many countries and people still live in poverty, and some even face the most basic problem of survival. In addition, along with the globalization process, many social problems such as the gap between the rich and the poor, environmental pollution, and education inequality are all urgently needed solving by the joined hands of human beings.

Domestically, since the reform and opening up, the advantages from policy, economy, and population have benefited generations of entrepreneurs for their rapid growth, and that is how private enterprises have sprung up one after another.

Nan Cunhui, chairman of Chnt Group, once said, "Reform and opening up has changed China and my destiny as well. Our courage and opportunity are given by the reform and opening up, so are our glory and dreams. It can be said that without this, there would be no China today. From this perspective, the material wealth of all Chinese businessmen and entrepreneurs is not their own but given by the great times and the great people.

In this context, we must make some difference as the beneficiaries of this great era. As conscientious businessmen and entrepreneurs, we should create and contribute rather than receive. First of all, we must continue to create material wealth and spiritual wealth. After that, we must continue to contribute both spiritual wealth and material wealth. Comparing the both, the latter is more important.

Someone commented on Bill Gates thus, "He has earned more than everyone else in human history. He is trying to donate money. Most people may have used their money elsewhere or donated only a little bit, in hopes of getting a medal, instead of spending all their time on something that really works as Bill Gates has been doing all his life."

According to Gates's donation program, his children can inherit only very little. After the departure of the couple, their personal wealth will be donated in return to all mankind. In 2010, while making his own donations, the Gates couple, together with Warren Buffett, launched a global initiative called The Giving Pledge through their social influence. The Pledge was meant for encouraging the wealthiest individuals and families around the world to invest most of their wealth in philanthropy to lessen the many pressing social issues that are most critical to the common destiny of mankind. In May 2019, according to the latest data, 19 philanthropists and families joined the initiative, including two from China.

The charity of these philanthropists deserves our respect. They have interpreted what is great love and benevolence. In fact, no real donation is meant for flowers and applause, nor for a show or vanity, but out of love and social responsibility that stem from "the thought of others from those in better conditions." "A rose given to another may leave its a fragrance in the giver's hand." For the donor himself, it is a joy to offer his wealth; for the whole society, it shows the power of a model role as a positive energy; for the whole country and even the whole world, it is a worthy thing that benefits the country and the people.

Many people have asked me why I donate. In fact, this is a decision made at the right time and at the right place. "Before your success, strive for self-cultivation; when in success, try to serve the world." At the company level, in the early days of my entrepreneurship, I was more concerned about my survival. After that, I needed to think about how to lead the company to take social responsibility and do what we could in return to the country, the Party and the society. On a personal level, all along the way, I have received selfless help from all walks of life. I have been deeply grateful for this.

In May 2017, after getting in contact with the University, I donated ¥16 million for the setup of funds for "Zeping Self-improvement Scholarship" and "Creation & Innovation" to reward and assist the hard-working and self-reliant students there, while fostering and supporting them for various innovations and entrepreneurship projects. In September, I donated ¥ 1.1 million to the High School affiliated to Southwest Jiaotong University, mainly for the improvement of its conditions and the support of their counterparts in the cultural education and targeted poverty alleviation work in Ma'erkang, Aba Prefecture. "The flames rise high when everybody adds fuel." The strength of one person is always insignificant. But as an ordinary Chinese youth, I wish my own story would find echo in more young people, and truly lead more substantial and talented youth with ideals to contribute to society and public welfare.

For the group of youth with the possession of more social resources, isn't this a great joy in life if this mission can be achieved at the critical moment when the Chinese nation strives for its great rejuvenation? We should make some difference and shoulder a national responsibility in the historical node of reform and development. Together, we will build the motherland and contribute all we are worth to the development of the motherland. When reliving this experience in old age, we will certainly feel that our life has been so valuable.

Poverty Relief & Measures

In alleviating poverty and getting rich, we have embarked on a road with Chinese characteristics and offered the world a Chinese plan in this aspect.

On the advent of the 70th anniversary of New China's founding and the 41st year of reform and opening up, let us look at such a set of data: From 2013 to 2018, China had exceeded the task of reducing poverty for six years on end. In the past 6 years, the country's cumulative poverty reduction population was 82.39 million, and the incidence of poverty fell from 10.2% to 1.7%. [1]

This set of data is a miracle of poverty alleviation not only in China, but also one in the history of world.

This is something in the world that can be done only in our socialist China. Living in such an era, under the leadership of such a party and government, young people should be more grateful and have a sense of national pride.

"People in poverty long enough should be relieved; and some benefits to them can

---

[1] Gu Zhongyang, Yu Jingwei,"China Has Totaled an Annual Poverty Reduction of 82.39 Million in Six Consecutive Years", http:// finance.china.com.cn/news/ 20190317/4925029.shtml.

reach the end." Right when the goal of achieving a comprehensive well-off society is approaching nearer, this hard battle against poverty is still going on. However, these flowers of change have already been in bloom in various regions.

Back this year to my birthplace, Fengcheng Town, Dazhou Prefecture, I witnessed the changes brought about there by targeted poverty alleviation. Most of the old villagers, poor and childless, have all been settled by the government in the nursing home and meticulously attended to for three meals a day. Meanwhile, a tarmac road has been built in the village where people live.

This is definitely a great era, quite subverting the way we used to live. For our hilly village of 1,500 meters above sea level, drinking water has been the hardest problem especially during drought. Though very thinlypopulated, the country has got a water storage tank ready there with water pipes connected to various households so tap water is accessible all year round.

In addition, excellent seeds such as rice and rapeseed are provided by the state free of charge. When a bumper harvest season comes but the labor force is insufficient, the villagers can report to the local government agencies for help. This is I have seen with my own eyes the results of targeted poverty alleviation.

Alleviating poverty has always been a worldwide problem. For the largest developing country on earth, it is an extremely difficult project. Based on more than 40 years' experience since China's reform and opening up, General Secretary Xi Jinping put forward the concept of targeted poverty alleviation, transforming the past flood irriga tion-type poverty alleviation into precise drip irrigation poverty alleviation, from blood transfusion poverty alleviation to today's hematopoietic poverty alleviation.

Poverty is not an unchangeable fate. There are no mountains higher than people, no road longer than the feet. In my hometown, the villagers have signed contracts on cash crops as agricultural resources with the corresponding enterprises through rural cooperatives. The sales market has been expanded and farmers' enthusiasm for production has become more motivated.

In more regions, the results of the hematopoietic targeted poverty alleviation are also marked. Teaching people to fish is better than giving them fish. The same is true of helping poverty education or developing other local industries. Poverty alleviation is indeed no charity, and guiding people with working ability to create a better tomorrow is the key to sustainable development.

"Getting rid of poverty is not just about getting rid of material poverty, but more about getting rid of poverty in consciousness and thinking. Wisdom against ignorance must go before fighting poverty." Poverty is less terrible than the lack of determination to change the status quo. Getting rid of poverty is not only for "a rich pocket", but also "a rich head."

As a grassroots entrepreneur who has struggled free from the countryside, I am deeply aware of the tremendous changes that "a rich head" has made. There are "five batches" of targeted poverty alleviation: the first by the development of production, the second by the relocation of poverty-stricken areas, the third by ecological compensations, and the fourth by the development of education and the fifth by the social security. Of all these, the fourth plays an important role. To enrich the head is to change the concept and raise the people's consciousness in poverty-stricken areas in various educational ways.

Lao Tzu once said, "It enriches you more to give others than to take from them." The same is true of an enterprise, so isn't it a reward for what one has paid? If a company's targeted poverty alleviation is well done, it reflects its vitality and enhances its reputation and popularity at the same time.

In March 2019, our company signed an agreement on targeted poverty alleviation.As one of the 48 enterprises in the high-tech zone, we will fully support Dege Village, one of the 48 in Ganzi Prefecture. After several meetings with local village Party chief, township head, our company will fully participate in it. After that, the infrastructure of the entire village, including roads and health centers, will be built by our company. We will organize a large amount of human and material resources to go deep into Dege's construction and do whatever possible to let the villagers live a happy and beautiful life.

A socialist country advocates common prosperity and allows some people to get rich first so that they will then lead more to get rich and finally achieve the great goal of common prosperity. Guided by the national policies, we should give full play to the strength of young entrepreneurs and at the same time play a leading role, and make more entrepreneurs help the poor and actively assume social responsibilities. Poverty alleviation must be supported and kept for some time. As a company involved in poverty alleviation, we should follow the country's efforts to focus on its next stage and pay attention to the follow-up development path of poverty-stricken areas.

No poverty alleviation should rebound, and the village should be kept on a healthy and sustainable upward growth.

The mission calls for responsibility, and it leads the future. As young entrepreneurs, we must hold high the great banner of patriotism and lend a great hand to the hard struggle for targeted poverty alleviation.

Education & Future

Here in the following is a passage by Tao Xingzhi, a people's educator, which expressed the importance of education to the development of the country, together with the key role of teachers in it:

"We firmly believe that education is a fundamental plan for the country; that education should foster vitality in students and make them grow up; that education should turn the resistance of the environment into a booster; that the life and work together between teachers and student make the best education; that teachers should lead as example; that teachers should learn and never tire of it; that teachers should develop their thinking and spirit of struggle by means of difficulties; that teachers should be friends to the people; that teachers, with the determination to die for educating the children, can create great new lives for our nation."

From ancient times till now, education has always been regarded as the country's heavy weapon. Good education is the hope of a nation and also a key to changing the destiny of an individual and a family and reshaping the individual's spiritual character.

Education is an extremely important matter for an individual, a family, a country and a nation. Education can change a person's destiny, especially the fair and just college entrance examination system. It can change a person's life path and break through his own limitations to usher in a different kind of scenery.

Imagine if there were no good education system or too few hardworking and selfless teachers, how could I, who had never been to kindergarten and missed the first two years at primary school, have entered Sichuan University? If I hadn't attended it, where could I be now?

But for education, a boy from the mountains would neither have had his literary dream at Peking University nor strongly desired better the conditions of his family and his own; he wouldn't have been helped by so many noble-minded people all the way nor grown into a young entrepreneur.

Therefore, when I was able to give something back to the society, I thought of education for the first time. It is hoped that, through donation, we will do our bit for the education in China so that a better education can be received by the future generations. My donation to society is mainly focused on education. The future transformation of my company to the media will be linked to cultural education. I have long been irrevocably committed to education, yet without my knowledge.

The country and the nation need education so much. Only when the education system keeps perfecting itself and stimulating people's potential can there be real hope for the national rejuvenation and the rise of the country. China needs to train more socialist successors to pass on the historically great mission and to take over the baton of their predecessors. Education needs the relay of people of insight, and more qualified young entrepreneurs are required to actively participate in education and make contributions to it. Only in this way can the future of the Chinese nation have real hope.

According to the statistics in 2019, 2018, there are 519,900 schools of all kinds throughout China, and 276 million students of various levels of education.

Today, nearly 20 million new children each year have become China's greatest resource. Only when China keeps its education in the strategic position of priority development, build a learning-type society, can a better tomorrow be created.

In the past 40 years of reform and opening up, the whole country has been advocating "knowledge is power". Since the restart of the college entrance examinations, 1.4 billion people have enriched their heads and pockets. Undoubtedly, education is still the most valuable and fulfilling public welfare undertaking. In the future, I will stick to this.

In the past 40 years of reform and opening up, China has achieved brilliant achievements that have attracted worldwide attention. One of them is education and talent. The resumption of the college entrance examinations, through the fair and just socialist education system, has enabled countless urban and rural youth to study hard, finally realize their values of life in new era and contribute to society.

However, as some people have got rich first, Chinese society has inevitably seen the phenomenon of an excessive gap between the rich and the poor. As a result, not a few people have begun to lament the solidification of the classes, jumped to the conclusion that "poor students can hardly emerge again."

This needs to be viewed dialectically, though. On the one hand, some families in superior conditions do occupy more and better education resources. On the other, those born in grassroots families can have more opportunities than ever. From the perspective of studying, China's education environment will get more and more fair. With the slanted national policies and related resources and the further development of rural education, educational undertakings in poor and backward areas will be upgraded to a considerable extent.

From the college entrance examination system, I still believe that this is the fairest exam the world over. Although it is like a thousand-strong horses crossing the wooden bridge, yet every year, many outstanding students are admitted to the university and receive high-quality education. Therefore, the channel for everyone to go up is always there. Besides, the state has a series of channels ready such as civil service examinations and postgraduate examinations. In the future, such channels will be more perfect and reasonable. Birth is not a fundamental condition that hinders individual growth and development. So long as one is down-to-earth, diligent and eager to learn, whether he chooses to study, get employed or start a business, he can amount to something. This being the case, education is there to serve as a social function for narrowing differences such as birth between people.

In 1922, Mr. Liang Qichao asked in a speech, "Why do you study?" "For learning to be a human. Courses like math, geometry, physics, chemistry, physiology, psychology, history, geography, Chinese, English, and even philosophy, literature, science, politics, law, economics, education, agriculture, industry or commerce are nothing but a means needed for that purpose. It cannot be said that relying on any of these can one achieve the purpose of being a human. Even when you are proficient in all these, whether you can be a real human is still a problem."

The essence of education is not to teach students how much knowledge and many professional skills, but to enable everyone to have a healthy and perfect personality, rich and sincere feelings, noble and upright virtues and the ideal goal to go beyond themselves.

Youth & Love of China

"Everyone is responsible for his country's rise or fall." In the long-standing spirit of the Chinese nation, the cultural genes that serve the motherland are always there. Militarily, Yue Fei got his back tattooed "loyalty to the country"; and literarily, Wen Tianxiang preferred death to surrender, which carries the same aspiration.

Patriotism, the foundation for young people to grow up and be useful, is the spiritual bond of the Chinese nation's united struggle and self-reliance for thousands of years.

As young entrepreneurs of the contemporary era, what should we do as we love our motherland?

We are fortunate enough to be born in a time of peace and prosperity, because we needn't shed blood, sacrifice, or kill ourselves as a sign of our devotion. Yet, as beneficiaries of this great era, more contributions to the motherland can be the very best way.

Why do I say so? It is based on three points: the social responsibility of an enterprise, the spirit of an entrepreneur, and the call by the great era. Any enterprise is based on profit, because it is the material basis for maintaining its survival and development.

Creating profits is important, but while doing so, the enterprise must have a sense of dedication and social responsibility. For an enterprise, as the pacesetter of a country's economic development and construction, getting most of the social wealth means assuming social responsibility. By doing so consciously, it benefits not only the country and the people, but also advances its own healthy and sustainable development.

There is no unified statement on the spirit of entrepreneurship. However, no matter how its connotations change, the courage to assume social responsibility and contribute more to the country should be an important part. No matter what era, the best embodiment of entrepreneurship is social responsibility.

Economy is the top priority of a country's development. In today's world, the problem that many countries are facing can run down to the economic problem. The entrepreneurial group is an important vitality for promoting the development of national economy.

Our eyes mustn't just be fixed on money. As entrepreneurs, we must bear the burden on our shoulders, and lift our feet so as to contribute to the development of our country. In this regard, "Glass King" Cao Dewang is our role model. Compared with his outstanding achievement in the field of automotive glass, people admire him more for his deed for charity. As "China's No One Philanthropist", he has donated ¥ 6 billion to the society, which is by far the most personal donation in China.

In addition, he insists that charitable projects must be implemented and practiced by specific people, doing charity in a good and thorough way.

In 2010, he donated ¥200 million to 100,000 poor families in the five southwestern provinces through the China Foundation for Poverty Alleviation. In order to ensure that the donations reached every recipient, he signed a very "harsh" donation agreement with the organization concerned: ¥ 200 million should be distributed to 100,000 farmers within half a year, and the error rate should be no more than 1%. If the Foundation should default, it must compensate. In addition, the management fee must not exceed 3% of the donation.

After signing the agreement, Cao also requested that the Foundation submit to him a project progress report every 10 days through the establishment of a supervisory committee of the news media. As a result, he has set a precedent for accountability for charitable donations in China.

In 2011, Cao handed over a total of ¥3, 549 billion worth of shares to his Heren Charity Foundation and created quite a few firsts such as the capital injection method, operation mode and management rules of the China Foundation.

When it comes to the spirit of entrepreneurship, he said, "From no action to actions, from a farmer to an entrepreneur, I have always been determined to follow the manufacturing industry, as a responsible entrepreneur. What is a responsible entrepreneur?

One who always regards the country's strength, social progress, and people's prosperity as his own responsibility, together with the sense of social responsibility and the determination to serve the motherland."

As young entrepreneurs, we must achieve something and, while contributing to the country, give full play to the entrepreneurial spirit of hard work and development for the enterprise.

What has made us entrepreneurs? It is absolutely inseparable from the national policy and the common support of the whole society. Therefore, when the enterprise is getting bigger and stronger, we should be grateful to and reward the motherland by doing social donations or volunteer work.

Just think, if a person keeps his head filled with money, he cannot hope to be a true entrepreneur. As entrepreneurs, we must set an example and encourage everyone else to take the road of entrepreneurial innovation, for one thing. For the other, we must encourage more people to be dedicated and self-reliant by taking the lead. If every entrepreneur does so, how can our motherland fail to be strong? How can the nation fail to be rejuvenated?

The power of a role model is endless for it can inspire more people to work harder. While promoting social material progress, entrepreneurship can gather a strong and positive energy in society and promote the progress of spiritual civilization.

The destiny of entrepreneurs is deeply connected with the country and the times, which creates great entrepreneurs. At present, it is a great era. When it comes to prosperity, we should be more self-reliant and achieve what is bestowed on entrepreneurs.

At the historic great stage of realizing the great rejuvenation of the Chinese nation and restarting of reform and opening up, and under the guidance of the "Belt and Road" and the strategy of targeted poverty alleviation, socialist young entrepreneurs should work together to contribute all their strength and wisdom to the country.

Contemporary young entrepreneurs, in addition to creating corporate wealth and expanding reproduction, are required to create material wealth and spiritual wealth for the country. In terms of material wealth, as its holders, we should take the initiative to assume social responsibilities and get more people to work and start businesses, realize the values of life, and contribute to the country and society. In terms of spiritual wealth, as young role models, we should convey the positive energy of society, establish a lofty ideal, shoulder the heavy responsibilities entrusted by the new era, and strive for the achievement of the Chinese Dream.

Part III

National Sentiment: Rise of Major Power and Road for Individuals

“One who intends for a long-term gain must aim high and see far.

Collected Works of Tang and Song Literary Giants. Ouyang Xiu, Ouyang Xiu of the Northern Song Dynasty”

A drop of water, only when merged into the sea, will not dry up. A flower, only when attached to its rhizome, will not wither. A person can achieve his ultimate value of life only by courageously fighting for the country and the times.

Throughout the ages, countless people with lofty ideals have deeply integrated their personal destiny with that of the country. While realizing their personal ideals, they have made great contributions to the country and the nation. Jia Yi, of the Western Han Dynasty, with his state in mind, repeatedly submitted his ideas on political affairs and wrote Public Security Policy, which has been deemed "the best political theory of the Western Han Dynasty." As a teenager, Zhou Enlai made up his mind to "Study for the Rise of China" on seeing the cruel reality of old China's being trampled upon by imperialist powers at will owing to its poverty and backwardness. Years after New China was founded, Lei Feng, a PLA man who served the people wholeheartedly, once said, "As the masters of the country, we should keep it at heart in every aspect."

The door to a new era is already open and China is now on its grand journey to realize the Chinese Dream of the great rejuvenation of the nation. As contemporary youth, we should inherit the sentiment for the homeland from our ancestors, break away from the narrow pattern of "little self", think about how to contribute more to the country and the people, and how to better combine our personal ideals with our country's future and destiny. The power of young people is endless. Over a hundred years ago, Liang Qichao said, "Beautiful is our China as young as the Heaven! And sturdy are our adolescents as long-living as the Motherland!" Young people, like the sun at eight or nine o'clock in the morning, are the hope of the country and the future of the nation. Now, the mission and heavy responsibility for reviving the nation and strengthening the country have fallen on us. We should take over the baton of our predecessors and lived up to what history has trusted on us by struggling onward.

07 Individuals & Country

To Carl Marx, the essence of mankind is the sum of all social relations. Individuals are always a product of a specific social situation. In terms of time, the survival and development of an individual cannot be separated from his era. In terms of space, he is inseparable from his country.

The opportunity of the times and the destiny of the country have a decisive and far-reaching impact on the fate of an individual. In this great and prosperous age, we young generation should follow the general trend and make some extraordinary achievements.

Individual Strength & National Strength

The times creates heroes. Each of us is a small individual in the era, which create conditions for our survival and development. However intelligent and strong a person is, he cannot show his talents and ambitions unless he follows the trend of the right times.

Lei Feng once said, “A drop of water, only when merged into the sea, will not dry up. A flower, only when attached to its rhizome, will not wither. A person can achieve his ultimate value of life only by courageously fighting for the country and the times.” Similarly, only by aiming high and striving in the ocean of the times can a person be most powerful.

The times create heroes and vice versa. In the face of the times, an individual can make some difference. In the case of a good one, he should make full use of the conditions given by the times, strive to realize the value of life, and make necessary contributions to the times and all mankind. When the times is bad, an individual will have to work hard, and contribute as he can to make it better.

From a global perspective, the theme of the present era is peace and development. After over one thousand years of war and strife, mankind has finally entered a historical stage of relative peace and stability. In this era, all countries have been availing themselves of the opportunity to focus on the development of their political, economic, cultural, scientific and other undertakings.

On the other hand, after a long period of historical evolution, mankind has gradually transitioned from primitive, agricultural, and industrial societies to present modern society, when it sees the fastest growing and highest level of productivity in history. In terms of material wealth and spiritual wealth, this is a very beautiful era.

Under the theme of this era of peace and development, individuals can not only enjoy a large amount of material wealth and spiritual wealth, but also create more for the times to realize the values and ideals of life using various conditions.

From the perspective of Chinese society, our generation is also very lucky. After the humiliation by the imperialist powers for above one hundred years and the arduous construction since the reform and opening up, China's comprehensive national strength has been greatly enhanced and its international status has increased remarkably. Currently, we are entering a new era of construction.

What is the construction of the brand-new era?

It is that of socialism with Chinese characteristics. Our country and nation have stood up, got rich, and strong from the history of its being humiliated and suppressed.

Only if the country is prosperous and strong, can it create a peaceful and prosperous development environment for individuals, and provide them with good development opportunities so that the people can work and live in peace and contentment.

Although the general trend of the world is still peace, yet in some corners of this world, discordant gunshots are still sounding from time to time. Imagine what would be the life for each of us without the peace and prosperity that the motherland supports.

Weak countries enjoy no diplomacy. One hundred years ago, at the Paris Peace Conference, the great powers ignored China's just request as one of the victors. They did not return to China its rights and interests to Shandong Germany had possessed, but instead transferred them to Japan, which humiliated China once again.

This greatly angered, Gu Weijun, the Chinese representative then. When he tried every means but in vain to win justice for the motherland, he announced his refusal then and there to sign the Treaty of Versailles. Later, he made a mention of this in his memoirs, "I am very disappointed. The Supreme Council ignored the existence of the Chinese people and sold China as a victorious country. I am angry, I am so indignant. What right do you have to give Japanese China's Shandong Province..."

In addition to the general background of the world, the strength of the country also determines the development of an individual's destiny. Without the strong motherland behind, no matter how good the world background is, it is a bad era for an individual. Only when the country is strong can the individuals be strong, and each of us be truly in the best times. In order for the humiliated history to not repeat itself, we must develop and strengthen ourselves in great earnest.

In this new era, what can we contemporary youth do?

As the new-era young Chinese placed in the great background of peace and development and at the key historical node of the Chinese nation achieving great rejuvenation and the restart of reform and opening up, what reason do we have for being pessimistic and slack?

In this era, what we fear is not failure but the waste of various advantages it has bestowed on us. This era has given us unlimited opportunities for creation, for hope and for thinking.

All in all, whether we start businesses, work or study, we should all be the runners and dreamers of this era. Each of us must do our best with our sleeves rolled up.

Ideal young people should struggle and create deeply in the torrent of the great times, making unremitting efforts to be worthy of our title as promising contemporary Chinese youth.

Power for China's Rise

Each era in history produces its talented people. Now, it seems to be the rule every hundred years for all countries. Portugal had risen from the Iberian Peninsula as the world's first global empire before replaced in turn by Spain, the Netherlands, France, and the United Kingdom.

Today, it has been more than 70 years since the United States became the world leader. At the upcoming 100-year junction, you may be wondering who will be the next leader?

The power for the rise of China, from a poor country to the world's second largest economy has amazed the rest world. New China was born "scarred" with a very weak economic foundation, yet it is worth focusing on the comparison of the past decades through a set of data by the National Bureau of Statistics: In 1978, China's national GDP was ¥ 364.52 billion, and its population totaled 96.259 million. The per capita GDP was only ¥ 381.23, ranking one of the world's last few, and by 2018, its annual GDP had reached ¥ 900.30 billion, its mainland population being 1.395 billion, and per capita GDP being ¥ 64,644, which is its economic total of ¥90 trillion for the first time, which means the world's second largest economy. [1]

All trades being thriving, the industrial structure was optimized and upgraded. In particular, Chinese farmers were no longer dependent on the weather for food. The total grain output had increased from 113.18 million tons right after the founding of New China to 657.89 million tons in 2018. The industrial development mode was no longer monotonous, but diversified, covering all the industrial types according to the UN Industry Classifications.

China's development path had been getting longer and longer. The visible road, namely, railway, had totaled 131,000 kilometers by the end of 2018, a five-fold increase over 1949, of which the high-speed railway was 29,000 kilometers, accounting for more than 60% of its kind in the world. The invisible road, namely, mobile broadband by 2018 had its users as many as 1.31 billion, the world's largest network being basically formed.[2]

During its great national rejuvenation, China has seen an earth-shaking change in its position around the globe. Today, all the eyes of the world have turned once again to it. Its comprehensive strength has been constantly increasing, and international status constantly improving, which has changed the world pattern in such few decades.

Then, what is the power that has enabled China to rise from its big fall, refresh its image as a major country in a short span of about 40 years, and achieve such a leap as a hundred times in total economic volume?

It was initiated in the new era of reform and opening up, based on the Party's long-

---

[1] National Bureau of Statistics, "China's Economic Operation is Generally Stable in 2018", https://baijiahao.baidu.com/s?id=1623322975113682883&wfr=spider&for=pc.

[2] "From a Poor and Blank Country to the World's Second Largest Economy, See What Has Happened in New China's 70 Years", http://m.news.cctv.com/2019/07/03/ARTIanHu2H9XcbMmqZx0zZV5190703.shtml.

term struggle and achieved by its generations of central leadership through uniting and leading the entire Party and people to experience hardships and pay all kinds of cost.

In the past, we have been under attack owing to our backwardness. Later on, we have chased and run all the way. Decades of hard construction, with the concerted efforts of the Party and the people, the tragic fate of China's domestic troubles and poverty since modern times has been reversed. At the moment of China's rapid rise, the Chinese nation, with more than five thousand years of civilization history, has finally re-established itself among the nations in the world.

Today, we have become a leader in many fields, and this is the power of China's rise. Now, as one looks up at this very country of ours, he will see its leading position that has penetrated into various industries.

In 2017, the venture capital data company CBInsights released the "2017 World's Most Valuable Unicorn List." Of the most valuable 197 "Unicorn" companies on the list, 49 were from China, accounting for 21%, and among the 15 super unicorn companies in the world, namely, of the "decacorn" companies, China had 6: Didi Chuxing, Xiaomi, Lufax, China Internet Plus Group, Today's Headlines and DJI- Innovation.[1]

In terms of distributions, the industries with the largest number of unicorns are in the fields of innovation, new and high-tech, and financial technology. These unicorn companies, born in the era of innovation, with their innovative thinking and global market competitiveness, are important fulcrums for national economic development and national rejuvenation, which means wealth, innovation, industry competitiveness and potential market space for prosperity.

---

[1] Mao Daqing,"Significance of Becoming a Unicorn is not to Monopolize, but Innovate", http://www.jjckb.cn/2017-11/01/ c_136719572. htm.

With the advent of the digital age, from the Internet of Things to the sharing economy, from the life economy to artificial intelligence, Chinese companies have a strong momentum of growth in both e-commerce and financial technology. Innovation has made the Chinese economy more internationally competitive. High-speed rail technology, global Alibaba and Huawei's 5G technologies have been known throughout the world, and China has begun to move toward the frontier of cashless society and smart countries.

At the key junction of the next century, which superpower will be the trend leader? Time will give us the answer.

Undoubtedly, as China is getting rapid change and development, we individuals should seize the opportunity and strive for our own rise.

Some people say that the group of Chinese entrepreneurs has grown up along with the great rejuvenation of the Chinese nation, for without the historical opportunity provided by the reform and opening up of 40 years ago, few of the untold entrepreneurs would have achieved so much today.

Today, as we young entrepreneurs are in a better era, namely, the restart of reform and opening up, the opportunity for individual rise is accompanied by an increase of the country's overall strength. How should we each seize the opportunity?

The youth of struggle is the best youth for seizing the opportunity.

Seizing the opportunity is the premise of struggle. Only by working hard and combining the ideal of life with the cause of the country can we make contributions to China in the new era.

Opportunities are always reserved for those who are fully prepared. If you are too conservative, sluggish, backward, and reluctant to move forward, life will leave you behind. Young people have great opportunities. Only when you continue to strengthen and arm yourself with abilities can you keep up with the opportunities by the times.

Marching with steady steps and being down-to-earth is the path under each and every one of us to realize our ideals of life. Despite so many opportunities, one cannot truly seize them unless he takes one steady step after another before writing his own life different from that of any others.

Today's world is no longer what it was 100 years ago. The power for China's rise, the world's second largest economy, has its influence on each of us Chinese. With its rise come more opportunities for individuals. In the face of the ubiquitous opportunities, just let our flower of youth bloom in profusion.

Era & Mission

The May 4th Movement is a grand festival for Chinese youth. Its spirit represents the magnificent and far-reaching dream of the Chinese youth and the hope of the country and the future of the nation.

What spirit does the Movement leave? Patriotism, progress, democracy, and science.

One hundred years ago, when China was beset with internal strife and foreign aggression, an anti-imperialist and anti-feudal patriotic movement broke out with the advanced youth as pioneers and the broad masses of all trades as the participants. As a result, the Chinese nation unveiled its prelude to a complete anti-imperialist and anti-feudal prologue. In this great movement, the Chinese youth were rushing here and there for saving the nation from peril, defending national dignity and uniting national power.

Regarding the strength of the May 4th youth, Li Dazhao once praised, "In the dictionary of youth, there is no such word as 'difficult' or 'obstacle' in their conversation;

they know only leap forward and bold flying and spirit of freedom as well as singular thought, sharp intuition, lively life for creating environment and overcoming history."

Now, just in the 100th anniversary of this event, we young people should do as the ancestors have done, carry forward the great spirit of the Movement, continuously infuse vitality into the times and constantly endow that spirit with fresh connotations.

In the new era, the Chinese youth should continue to carry forward the great spirit of the May 4th Movement and fulfill the great rejuvenation of the Chinese nation as expected by the Party, the nation and the times.

Since China's reform and opening up, its economic strength has rapidly increased and overall national strength continuously strengthened. Today, when socialism with Chinese characteristics has entered a new era, the nearest time for realizing the great rejuvenation of the China and the goal of building a prosperous, strong, democratic, civilized and harmonious socialist modern country is just in view.

With the times comes its mission. The Chinese youth are promising and will surely be so, as the hope of the nation. Being the backbone of building the nation in the new era, we must strive for self-improvement, fully display our pioneering role and grow more capable.

Then, as the master of this new era, and as an ideal young person, how will you plunge yourself deep into the torrent of the national rejuvenation through your struggle and creation? In the context of a brand-new era, how should we rekindle the burning spirit of the Movement?

Rekindling its soul, contemporary young people should be the top runners of the times. Whether in entrepreneurship, employment or learning, we should exert ourselves.

We, young people of this era, must have lofty ambitions and ideals, and have deep feelings for our country, and merge our own personal ideals into those for realizing the great rejuvenation of the nation.

Relying on the great background of progress of the times, we young people must each contribute our bit to the great rejuvenation of the Chinese nation while developing and upgrading ourselves; we must make great strides forward, respond to the call of the times, "roll up our sleeves and work hard", and carry on the mission of the new age.

Rekindling its soul, we contemporary youth must have the spirit of and tenacious will for shouldering the mission. "Whoever meant for the important tasks placed by the Heaven will first be made to suffer mental pain, physical tiredness and bodily starvation." The great rejuvenation of the nation is no easy task. As the backbone of this era and the hope of national development, we youth people must constantly enrich and elevate ourselves, thoroughly study and implement General Secretary Xi Jinping's six hopes for the Chinese youth in the new era, establish a lofty ideal, love our great motherland, take responsibility for the times, dare to struggle, hone hard skills, and cultivate morality.

As young entrepreneurs, we must constantly integrate national development with individual ideals and keep up with the trend of the times. In the process of the continuous development and mingling of Asian civilization with world civilization, China Colorful Civilization Development Foundation we intend to initiate in the future, will be rooted in Asia and oriented to the world to fulfill our mission as the inheritor, champion and contributor of civilization.

Among them, the mission for my team is to promote Chinese civilization and tell the Chinese story to the world. To this end, we will build a world-class cultural media group and in the future, and gradually build an overseas development strategy platform, so as to enable the world to hear more of the Chinese youth and feel more of its charming culture. Meanwhile, I will fulfill my share of the social responsibility I should, exhaust my wisdom and strength to do a good job of public welfare for China and the rest world.

Whether the company will go public or not is not our dream, but a process instead; making money is not our goal, but a data instead. For the young generation, the ultimate goal and ideal of wealth creating is to contribute to Chinese culture, Asian culture and even world culture for more people, which is our mission.

As young people born in this age, we are lucky enough compared to our predecessors. Now, we own their spiritual legacy, a stable environment, opportunities for development, and a prosperous country. What other reasons do we have for being lax? At a time when the goal for realizing the great rejuvenation of the Chinese nation is getting closer and closer, we should participate in and contribute to it, and press forward on the basis of the inheritance by the predecessors. This is what we contemporary young people should do. China's revival has reached a best era, providing us with unlimited opportunities and hope. All in all, the times is calling, and it is time for us to take over the mission.

Two Centenary Goals & Chinese Dream

In the past 40 years of reform and opening up to the outside world, China has undergone earth-shaking changes. Both the level of national economic development and the people's living standards have been significantly improved. And China is now the world's second largest economy.

Die Welt once commented, "In no country but China, individuals can so quickly create large amounts of wealth in the socialist market economy."

"Where the Spring breeze arrives, every plant revives." Today, we are in a good time where everyone can have and fulfil their dreams.

Everyone has their dreams and pursuits, or visions and desires. Now, the Chinese Dream has become a dream on the lips of everyone. What is it? General Secretary Xi Jinping defined that "the realization of the great rejuvenation of the Chinese nation is the greatest dream of the Chinese nation in modern times" and expressed that it is now "we are closer to the goal, more confident in and better capable of realizing the great rejuvenation of the Chinese nation than at any time in history." This very Dream requires that generations of Chinese people take over the baton and work together for it. As contestants of this relay race in this era, we should all strive for this great dream.

We are all familiar with the "Two Centenary Goals". In the first one, when the Communist Party of China ushers in its 100th anniversary (2021), China will be built into a well-off society in an all-round way; and in the second one, when China ushers in its 100th anniversary (2049), it will be a socialist modern country, which is rich, democratic, civilized, harmonious and beautiful.

The goals above to be striving for and the Chinese Dream complement each other as the call of the times to lead China forward.

Everyone's future and destiny are closely linked to that of the country. When the country is strong, the individual is strong. As young entrepreneurs, we better understand that, as a tiny molecule of the social cycle, the development of an enterprise is inseparable from the support of all sectors of society, nor is from the good business environment created by the Party and the Government.

In the past 40 years of reform and opening up, China has "hatched" too many entrepreneurs and created too many myths of wealth. Imagine that without the great policy of reform and opening up, or the vast market of China's 1.4 billion people, could entrepreneurs such as Yu Minhong and Ma Huateng have been as they are today? Could I have left my mountain village for realizing the dream as an entrepreneur?

The realization of the Chinese Dream needs the power of all of us brought together. As a member of the country, one of the Chinese entrepreneurs, doing our bit for the Chinese Dream is a common responsibility for each of us.

Zong Qinghou is one of my most admired business leaders in China. His great feelings for the country, attitudes and deeds to help its development are definitely great examples.

As the founder of Wahaha Group, he started from scratch, and got on the Forbes Fortune list three times and ascended the throne of the richest man in the Chinese mainland in 2010, 2012, and 2014 respectively. However, what he wins my greatest respect is not his wealth, but his constant sentiments for the country.

In 2013, Zong Qinghou, at a motion release meeting in Beijing, responded solemnly to the long-circulated rumor concerning his "green card issue" before a group of reporters, "I have no other nationalities, or green cards, nor will I be an emigrant in the future. Because I know no foreign language or adapt to any foreign food. I have no interest in staying abroad. I live very well in China. I have my career here, so I will never be an emigrant."

At the historical stage of the restart of reform and opening up, as Chinese entrepreneurs and the youth, we should share such a sentiment of his. No matter how big my future business goes, I will always hold on to that sentiment myself and never be an emigrant.

Personal dreams are linked to the Chinese Dream. One excellent entrepreneur, industry elite and technical backbone after another have injected his inexhaustible power into that Dream. Now, our efforts for it have already shown results.

In 2015, CSR and CNR were formally merged into China CRRC Co., Ltd., which will promote the transformation of "Made in China" to "Created in China".

In 2018, Chinese Internet giants Tencent and Alibaba ranked among the top ten most valuable brands in the world, with Tencent being second only to Google, Apple, Amazon and Microsoft. [1]

In 2019, Huawei took the lead in the 5G field. Fortunately for China, the R & D capability of this product has won the highest honor and got recognized in the national quality field, which means a historic transformation of a Chinese company.[2]

From "making" to "creating", from "OEM" to "name brand", from "following" to "leading" in partial areas, this is the full expression of promoting the national spirit, pooling the China's strength and realizing the Chinese Dream.

As young people with a global outlook, we will all start businesses around the world in the future, find like-minded partners, and even invest there.

Today, with the daily acceleration of globalization, enterprises and technology without borders will gradually reach a consensus. However, as the new entrepreneurs, we should carry on the glorious tradition of the older generation, resist all temptations at the critical moment, and shoulder the national burden and national responsibility. We must create wealth in all walks of life for the motherland and even the entire human race.

The Chinese Dream is the result of the great journey of arduous explorations for the road to creating socialism with Chinese characteristics.

Looking back at the early days after the founding of New China, the people of the

---

[1] "From Chinese Manufacturing to Chinese Creation, China's National Brand Value Ranks Second in the World", Https://finance.china.com/domestic/11173294/20181015/34161600.html.

[2] Sun Like, *A Biography of Ren Zhengfei*, Zhejiang People's Publishing House, 2017.

whole country, under the leadership of the Party, worked hard to build a prosperous and socialist modern country.

Today, we are working hard for the Chinese Dream. For the second centenary goal, we will continue our march forward on the road of socialism with Chinese characteristics. The reform and opening up has taken us on the path of rapid development. We are closer to the realization of the "Chinese Dream" than any period in history.

Youthful ideal, vitality, and struggle are the Chinese spirit and the power of China. As young people and young entrepreneurs, each of us must strive for our own dream and Chinese Dream and work hard to achieve the great rejuvenation of the Chinese nation.

08 Start of New Era & Belief of Chinese Youth

The new era, new mission, and new dreams call for the new generation of young people to bravely go on the road.

As the young Chinese of the new era, we must make a difference by following the general trend of the times. At the key point of the great rejuvenation of the Chinese nation and the restart of reform and opening up, we should grow up as early as possible in practice as dreamers with faith, hardship, and mission.

Power of Belief & Reform

The power of spiritual belief is very strong for both individuals and the collective. On the 25,000-li Long March, the Chinese Red Army soldiers snatched the Luding Bridge by force, crossed the Dadu River, climbed the snow-capped mountains, covered the grass... all thinly clad, eating in the wind and sleeping in the dew. Despite the enemy fires from all around, the older generation still held on with clenched teeth, relying only on the great ideal of overthrowing the old world for the building of a new China.

The French Literary Giant Victor Hugo once said, “Belief is what people need. People without it will not get happiness.” Belief is where a soul can perch itself. Without this, no one can be complete, after all. Neither his emotions, nor words, nor deeds can have the thickness of the soul.

It is relatively easy for a person to have a belief, and it is much harder for a large group to share the same belief. Even if it is reached temporarily, how to key it for long is a test of the collective wisdom of the organization.

However, if all members of an organization have that shared spiritual belief in a certain period of time, unite and work together for it, they will get tighter and tighter as a rope does, and constantly release an invincibly powerful energy.

A review shows how our previous revolutionaries have gone through the years of Resistance War Against Japan despite life and death. Having experienced that difficult period of poverty and hardships, they had proposed the great decision on the reform and opening up when national power was still weak.

The power of belief supports the progress of the Chinese nation from generation to generation. Today, in this new era, we still cherish the same belief and strive for the great rejuvenation of the Chinese nation.

At age 18, I was fortunate enough to join the Chinese Communist Party with a lofty ideal and became one of the two youngest party members throughout the University that year. Since my ten years of party membership, this revolutionary power has accompanied me, and the hard work has encouraged me up to now.

Today, the role of spiritual belief can never be ignored. For the young generation, what kind of person can be our model role in life? I think that people with a pure heart and patriotism are the real “stars”.

The growth of either a nation, an enterprise, or an individual can go with the power of belief. Its correct leading role will be as mighty as the power of a landslide and a tidal wave. While believing in its power in the torrent of reform, we must guide the life of the contemporary youth with positive energy and red culture.

Under the influence of such a belief, we must internalize the slogans of “Work hard with our sleeves rolled up”, “We are all dreamers” and “Be the vanguards of the times” and join the new and young Chinese who are hardworking and enterprising. Let the magnificent, honest and red belief accumulate and deepen itself, and inspire us to be role models for others in work and life.

As contemporary young entrepreneurs, how do we internalize the power of belief into the enterprise and pass it on to the other youth of the company?

I am the beneficiary of the revolutionary belief, knowing that it can bring an inexhaustible power. Just after our company was set up, the Party group was established, so the Party building was rooted in the corporate culture and became the "red engine" for its development.

On the walls of the company compound are the 100 model roles we have advocated. Walking around, you will see Qian Sanqiang, Yuan Longping, Yang Zhenning, Zhan Tianyou, Qu Yuan, Li Bai, Du Fu and others.

Today, with the continuous development and progress of the times and society, the construction of Party organizations in enterprises is becoming more and more important. The Party building work is not only unique to state-owned enterprises, but to all non-public ones for their own Party building activities according to their own conditions.

On the one hand, we entrepreneurs should continue our exemplary roles, promote entrepreneurship, be brave in innovation, keep making progress, and transform the spiritual power of Party building into the infinite vitality for enterprise development. On the other, we must carry through our love for the Party, the prosperity for the Party, and the protection of the Party in all aspects of business management, dare to take and fulfill our responsibilities, serve the society, and actively participate in all major strategies of the country.

Follow the revolutionary torrent for building the core belief of the company. With the continuous development of the enterprise, we should constantly perfect the relevant

Party organization structure, and form the labor union and service team of volunteers, so that the Party building work can be deeply rooted in the corporate culture and become a true “red engine” for the development of the enterprise.

Talent is the key to the development of society and enterprises. Therefore, within my enterprise, the training mechanism cannot be ignored. Construction of the Party member team is the foundation in the enterprise organization, which concerns its development and reform. When the company was established, I began to carry out the dual cultivation mechanism of “training Party members into excellent employees and excellent employees into qualified Party members.”

This mechanism not only pushes the grass-roots Party organizations to the forefront for the development of advanced productive forces, but also absorbs the outstanding talent of the enterprise into the Party.

Under the dual cultivation mechanism, all Party members within the company have played the role of vanguards and model roles, which prompts more employees to learn from them, and the whole team has become united and enterprising. At the very beginning, I was only the Party member in the company. Through this mechanism, we have encouraged the cultivation of activists to join the Party and turned outstanding Party members into outstanding talent.

Be the vanguard of the times. Our company regularly organizes the study of the important speeches by General Secretary Xi Jinping. By exchanging ideas, we have learnt how to transform spiritual power into corporate vitality and promote enterprise development and progress.

The revolutionary power is the spiritual driving force that supports the hard work of the older generation. Concentrating this power can help promote the healthy development of an enterprise, so we have carried out the red activities such as love for the

Party and the country, self-reliance and self-strengthening. Reviewing the history of the Long March and that of reform and opening up can enable us younger generation to remember history and strengthen the power of beleif.

Today, in the new era of China, the red culture is injected into the enterprise development, which promotes its growth. Within the company, each employee can sing at least 10 red songs and has read 10 revolutionary books; we have organized employees for red tourism to Liangjiahe besides the former residences of Deng Xiaoping and Mao Zedong. Under the influence of this culture, we have been rid of impetuosity and worked even harder.

As a Party member of more than ten years, I have been encouraged and helped up to now step by step by the power of this belief.

Today, I believe that the power of belief should be raised as to be in step with the times. When this red power and culture has been constantly passed on and learned, a strong torrent of positive energy can be formed between people.

The young are strong, so will the country be. We should follow the revolutionary tide, trust in the power of belief, and help the other Chinese youth to forge ahead. Let the revolutionary and vigorous force get gradually accumulated and deepened, so as to inspire us youth all to strive to be role models in their work and life.

Hard Workers as "Key Minority"

In the winter of 1962, Jiao Yulu reached Lancao County, Henan, only to see it visited by such prevalent "three evils" as waterlogging, sandstorm and land salinization. He willingly bore the burden of office by fighting against them with the local people even when he had liver cancer, hence the "Spirit of Jiao Yulu".

Later, his health condition worsened. While in sickbed, he urged, "Take me back to Lankao and bury me on a sandpile. I have failed to overcome the sand dunes, so let me see you make it." On May 14th, 1964, Jiao Yulu died of illness at 42.

"I won't rest content until I can benefit the place where I work as an official."

The core spirit of the "key minority" is hard work, the tradition of the Communists. In the historical development track of our Party, either from the war years to the establishment of New China, or to the new stage of reform and opening up, the main theme behind every development is hardship and hard work.

Looking back on my career of over a decade as a Party member, I have been deeply touched by this hard-working tradition of the Communists.

I am a young entrepreneur and a Communist as well. For the country, only by displaying the role of "key minority" as Party members who are leading cadres, and advancing the spirit of hardiness, can we serve the people heart and soul. For the enterprise, it is to work hard in the ordinary position, and to focus on the work to be done in a solid manner. At the same time, it is necessary to give play to the exemplary role of a Party member within the company and make extraordinary things in his ordinary position.

The "key minority" is the steering wheel for the enterprise development. In the contact with my peers from all walks of life, I have very keenly felt that in a company with stronger strength and better management, its work regarding Party building has been carried out very well without exception and all Party members as the "key minority" have all been hard-working model roles.

Among the team, the Party members should be the "key minority" who are more responsible, have more ideals and can better bear hardships and more often take the lead as pace setters. In 2016, our company moved toward diversification and entered in the media sector. In the face of a new industry, new equipment and new technology, everyone in my R & D team, half of it being Party members, thought about and did the same thing and, reducing original three-month R & D cycle to half a month, seized the market opportunity.

Today, with China's national rejuvenation and its rise as a major country, the opportunities, markets and policy environment that Chinese entrepreneurs have are unparalleled. In the best of times, we must display our role of hard work and struggle and take the lead in being the "key minority" Party members and leading cadres. We must actively cultivate talented personnel with high ideological qualities highly identified by the masses, and restore a reserve army for the enterprise development, so that the whole team can form a positive and enterprising atmosphere.

In the enterprise, everyone should strive to be one of the "key minority" by taking over the dirty and tiring jobs and leaving the rest it to the majority; be enterprising in what we are after, work hard at the post; and be willing to contribute in daily life, and form a powerful red torrent of positive energy in a quiet way.

An excellent Party member must have this spirit of bearing hardship and working hard. As members of the Party, we should know that our ancestors had undergone hardships and hard work before they ushered in New China.

There is no reward without previous efforts. What hardships and hard work bring us is the enrichment and improvement of knowledge, skills and experience. At the same time, it is the power of role models that drives more people to develop excellent qualities of hardship and hard work.

As outstanding Party members, we should work hard to create a beautiful life, and take the initiative as pacesetters and demonstrators. We will work hard so as to make hardiness the prevailing practice, unite the power of thousands of others for achieving the great rejuvenation of the Chinese nation.

As young entrepreneurs, we should never forget our aspiration, but move forward, integrate personal dreams with social responsibilities, and carry forward the spirit of the "key minority".

In 2007, I, with little knowledge in aquaculture, ventured into the tide of entrepreneurship and worked hard for my life with a powerful spiritual force guiding me.

Learn everything new little by little from scratch. Isn't this the quality of hard work? If a 19-year-old boy could do it one step after another, he would make a representative for college students in self-reliance. You can do the same for the Chinese youth in the new era.

Even at the moment when I fell into the bottom of misery, I kept reminding myself that there was no desperate situation in the world, but the desperate state of mind, kept with the fine qualities of hardship and endurance shown by the Communists, and finally reversed my conditions.

When doubted by most people, I still firmly adhered to my ideal and belief, stuck to my choice of entrepreneurship, and finally helped and led more aspiring young people bravely onto the same road as hard fighters for their own life.

The times will never let down the hard-working people. An outstanding communist and a representative of young entrepreneurs, must give full play to his leading role as one of the "key minority", be willing to endure and look hardships in the face, be good at merging his hardships into daily life, so as to be an example and pacesetter for everyone else.

The "key minority" is a key word for governing a country. Only when those "key minority" take the lead can they produce the "head goose effect". The mastery of "key minority" is the mastery of both responsibility and example.

For the state or the enterprise, grasping the "key minority" is to grasp the focus of development. Today, as the socialism with Chinese characteristics has entered the new era, the responsibility by the "key minority" is even more important. Each of us youth should strive to be an example and one of the "key minority" and hand in a beautiful answer for the development of the times.

Aspiration & Mission

"I dreamed that our rice was growing as tall as the sorghum with each of its ears as long as the broom and each grain as big as a peanut. My assistants and I were enjoying the cool under the ears of rice..." This dream of rice has been in Yuan Longping's mind for decades.

In 2005, the UN World Food Program officially announced that it would stop food aid to China from 2006. Since then, China's 26-year history of food aid has received a full period, and instead it has begun to donate food to the outside world. In this process, the hybrid rice developed by Yuan has been playing a decisive role. After the advent of hybrid rice, China has supported 20% of the world's population with less than 10% of its cultivated land, making such a great contribution to the elimination of hungry population throughout the world.

To get the Chinese well fed, Yuan Longping, together with his assistants, worked on rice hybridization experiments. Through plenty of hardships, he has finally found a sterile plant in Hainan, China. After that, he and his team spent six full years using more than 1,000 varieties to make more than 3,000 hybrid combinations. None of them had nurtured rice seedlings with an infertility of 100%.

One will make it if he bears in mind his aspiration. After overcoming countless difficulties in 1973, he published a paper entitled "Advances on Selection of 'Three

Lines' with Wild Rice", officially proclaiming his success of the Indica "three-line" hybrid rice. Under his unremitting persistence, China's food security has been guaranteed, and the human problem of feeding has been solved.

In any age, young people are the hope and future of the country. We must bear in mind our mission entrusted by history and our aspiration as well. Since his youth, Yuan has never forgotten his historical mission. Therefore, he has worked hard day and night and finally developed hybrid rice.

Today, there are so many fine examples around us who keep in mind their aspiration and mission. For instance, the people's police, white angels of medical workers, journalists, bus drivers and so on. They put the people's interests above all else. With the mission entrusted by the country and history at heart, they have done brilliant jobs in all walks of life, working hard and struggling for the Chinese Dream of the great rejuvenation of the Chinese nation.

The aspiration and the mission may refer to one's persistence in difficulties and setbacks, his clear head before temptation, his firm belief or indestructible light on the road ahead. This is not only the mission of the ordinary Chinese, but also a lifelong task for Communists.

As Communist Party members, we must always remember our aspiration and mission. I will constantly do so while leading the Lanjiao Media steadily on a new journey and do more influential things. As a name card for the Chinese youth, I should shoulder my share of the national mission and responsibility. Through China Colorful Civilization Development Foundation that is being prepared, I will promote the exchange and cooperation of Asian civilization, and better convey Chinese culture and tell Chinese stories to foreign friends on the world stage.

From nothing to the comprehensive company group of some scale and influence, Lanjiao Media has never been separated from the help of people from all walks of life, and from the concern and support of the Party and the country. It can be said that all its achievements have been endowed by the Party and the state, so we will create more values for society and the country.

We insist on normalizing our activities of learning and "brain enriching", doing an in-depth study of the Party's knowledge and "Xi Jinping Thought on Socialism with Chinese Characteristics for the New Era" and regulating our own words and deeds with the standards for Party members. I believe in the great power of this red engine. The establishment of belief requires a "smooth and silent" process. "Belief in what we are after" is the aspiration of Lanjiao Media. We have always insisted on it while moving forward in great earnest with our love for, belief in, protection of the Party.

Over the past seven years, Lanjiao Media has been insisting on its aspiration. Stress on our belief and red culture has gradually made each of our employees familiar and from very little to very much knowledge with them. In the end, the great power generated by this unforgettable red engine has begun to influence everyone in the group company. In its future development, I believe that the continued explosive power of this red engine will be incalculable and keep active the entire Media.

Everyone who is busy in their own walk of life, who seriously lives in their life, who marches bravely against the tide... from an ordinary individual dream to the great Chinese Dream, as long as we don't forget our aspiration and work hard, we will be able to see the Dream come true sooner or later.

The Chinese youth have their own responsibility while enjoying their beauty of youth. We have our ideals, vitality and courage for innovation, which is make the power for the rise of China.

The Chinese youth have their own responsibility while enjoying their beauty of youth. We have our ideals, vitality and courage for innovation, which make the power for the rise of China.

All along, the great national spirit with patriotism as its core of unity and solidarity, peace-loving, diligence, courage and self-reliance has inspired generations of Chinese. The Chinese nation has been standing erect in thousands of years, and continuously gathering the majestic power of national rejuvenation. That is why we have already been on the road of national rise and rejuvenation.

China boasts a bright future. With our aspiration, mission and unremitting efforts, we will surely be able to usher in the day when our grand blueprints are all realized.

Responsibility for the Era

The new era with its new atmosphere also calls for new actions. At present, the building of socialism with Chinese characteristics has entered a new era. This is the new historical orientation for China's development.

Where is the new era new?

At present, the main contradiction in our society has been transformed into the one between the people's growing needs for a better life and the development of inadequate imbalances. This major contradiction has marked the historical changes in the overall development of our country and has put forward many new requirements for the development of various tasks.

In the future, building a well-off society in an all-round way and building a strong, modernized, and socialist country in an all-round way will be the historical mission and strategic arrangement of the new era.

Specifically, when the socialist modernization is basically realized in 2035, all the people will move toward common prosperity at a solid pace. By mid-21th century, when China is built into a strong, democratic, civilized, harmonious, beautiful and modernized socialist country, the common prosperity for all people will be basically realized.

At present, in terms of economic development, with the booming of emerging industries, China's traditional industries have accelerated their transformation and upgrading. With the wide spread of mass entrepreneurship and innovation, the technology-led economic development model has been initially established in China. This shows that in the new era, China's economy has broad prospects for development.

This Dream is not only a national dream, but also a personal dream, not only the present dream, but also the eternal dream throughout history and the future.

On the world stage, with the constant rise of its international status, China plays an increasingly important role in international affairs. The solution to international problems is increasingly inseparable from China's participation.

What kind of new era is this for us young people?

It is such a good era that everyone has the opportunity to realize their dream and become a tide rider. The rapid development of information technology has really made the world as small as a global village.

You can really feel that the changes around you, and the rejuvenation of the Chinese nation are within sight:

Its space dream is getting bigger and bigger. In 2019, Chang'e No. 5 will realize the first return to China after its lunar sampling. This space launch mission is technically difficult and complex, and it is a key step in completing the lunar exploration project "rounding, landing, and returning". The Beidou satellite navigation project will complete the 7-Arrow 10-Star launch mission to prepare for the full completion of global networking in 2020. In addition, Long March No.11 sea launch and Jielong No.1 commercial launch vehicle will achieve the first flight, and the cumulative number of launches of the Long March series will exceed 300 times.

Our dream of high-speed rail is getting bigger and bigger. After ten years of development, its high-speed rail operating mileage in China has reached 29,000 kilometers, surpassing two-thirds of the world's total. At present, China has become the one with the longest high-speed rail, highest transportation density and most complicated network operations in the world. As China's high-speed rail speeds continue to rise, the convenient life brought by it has covered 180 prefecture-level cities and more than 370 county-level cities across the country.

In addition, the development of technologies such as aircraft carriers and artificial sun shows a good trend, and artificial intelligence and 5G era are already waving to us. Now, China's new four inventions such as high-speed rail, scan code payment, shared bicycle and online shopping are going global, and more and more profoundly influencing people's life in the world.

Since 1990, China has sent more than 39,000 peacekeepers, participated in the road construction project of over 13,000 kilometers in the peacekeeping areas, received more than 170,000 patients, and completed more than 300 tasks such as armed patrol patrols. Among them, the Chinese Navy's 'Peace Ark' Hospital has visited 43 countries, benefiting more than 230,000 locals.

In diplomacy, China has been consistently pursuing an independent policy and made positive contributions to resolving international disputes, regional conflicts and combating terrorism. Today, China has become an important force for maintaining world peace and stability, and successfully established its image in the world as a responsible major country.

The new era has opened a new chapter, and China is moving towards a new journey. We have ushered in a new era of a great leap from standing up, getting rich to getting strong, in a new era in which China contributes wisdom to world peace and development, and a new era of more attention to balance under the guidance of new development concepts.

What kind of mental state should the Chinese youth have in the new era? What ambitious goal for them to achieve?

A country thrives if its youth do so; a country is strong if its youth are so. In the new era, we are facing new opportunities as well as new challenges. At present, we must brave the tide, dare to take the lead, and struggle with our sleeves rolled up! On the road of struggle, we need to remember our aspiration, work practically, love the Party and the country, be self-reliant, create values, and contribute to society!

In the new era, we must keep in step while clear about its new requirements. The new era calls for a new look and requires us to constantly create new achievements. "With a confident life span of two hundred, I can swim three thousand miles ahead." We must establish a lofty ideal, love the great motherland, dare to take responsibility for the times, courageously struggle on, hone hard skills, and cultivate morality.

"Idle boast the strong pass is a wall of iron, with firm strides we are crossing its summit." The wheel of history is rolling forward, the trend of the times is vast, the grand blueprint of the new era has been drawn up, and the great journey of the new era has begun. Our prospects are bright though challenges are very severe.

The dream of over one billion Chinese has been transformed into the Chinese

Dream of a new era. We believe that it will be realized. All Chinese youth will be bravely marching toward the goal with a spirit of perseverance and a persistent stance and strive to create a new situation for the Chinese Dream.

09 Innovators' Exploration

"If you can in one day renovate yourself, do so from day to day. Yea, let there be daily renovation."

Innovation, for the individual, is a bold breakthrough from the comfort zone; for the enterprise, it is the key to life and death; for the country and nation, it is an important prerequisite for strength and prosperity.

The journey to innovation, rather than smooth sailing, is always difficult and accompanied by various challenges. However, innovation is a must. As young people of the new era, we must be brave to innovate, boldly break away with old things, and then create new ones.

Innovation Doomed Tough

Innovation is an unknown adventure. In this process, you must have the courage to smash some old conventions, which may harm the interests of some people, and challenge the established understanding of most people. Not all innovations will succeed. If your innovation is not in line with the needs of the times, it will be questioned and opposed by people and then fail. Therefore, innovation is doomed to be a hard process, whether successful or not.

Why do enterprises and entrepreneurs now keep talking about innovation? Because in this era of traditional industries receiving continuous transformation and innovation, they have a strong sense of crisis, and are vying with each other for innovation in institutions, products, technology, and so on. So this road to innovation is destined to be far from ordinary and smooth.

Despite the difficulties, innovation is imperative and must be done either for the country, the enterprise or the individual.

Let's take Haier for example. When reform and opening up just began in China, many enterprises only paid attention to the amount of production. Haier took the lead in proposing to implement total quality management, and smashed the old concept of "special, first-class and second-class products". After that, it took the lead in implementing innovative measures such as Diversified Development Strategy and OEC Management (Overall Every Control and Clear). Even after China's entry into the WTO, Haier still insisted on the concept of its "going out being not for earning foreign exchange, but more important for creating China's own brands", adopted the "three-step" strategy of "going out, going in, going up", followed the idea of "being difficult before being easy", from developed to developing countries, and gradually established overseas a localized model of "three in one" in design, manufacturing and marketing.

In the Internet era, Haier has embarked on the road of user-centered service and is committed to becoming a platform-based enterprise. Now, "Haier is transforming from an organization that originally manufactured products into an accelerated platform for incubating makers." Along the way, Haier, always able to innovate and stay ahead of others in the market, has prevented itself from bankruptcy owing to heavy debts and now turned into a global home appliance brand from a collective small factory.

For Haier, the fruits of innovation are rich and sweet, but the process is fraught with difficulties. In his book *Haier's History of Innovation*, Zhang Ruimin described the difficulties encountered when he started innovation, "Since 2005, Haier has been exploring person-order win-win mode by trial and error. For this reason, we abandoned with no hesitation the single pursuit of traditional performance. In the absence of unmarked groping, we would rather endure outside doubts and criticisms than give up."

For the enterprise, every innovation can be either an opportunity for development or an insurmountable hurdle.

With the change of the macroeconomic situation, China's economy has entered into a new normal, and all trades have begun to adjust, transform or upgrade themselves, my company being no exception. A few years ago, upon some careful considerations, I made up my mind to re-adjust the company's strategic layout, and shut down industries such as electronics, house decorating, and communications. In the face of this sudden adjustment, many veteran employees found it difficult to accept for some time, because electronic communication was my start-up and most profitable industry. Many employees had been doing so well, loved it so much with great pride. Although I had repeatedly told them about my strategic intention of doing so, they eventually chose to leave for lack of understanding.

I started house decorating soon after that. In order to encourage every employee, I had drawn a new blueprint for the company's industrial development, drafted a very ambitious decorative dream for them, and tried to build the company into a decorative empire. But for the company's strategic development, I had to turn it off. It was something so cruel, and the employees felt so wronged at the time, thinking that their labor was neither respected nor protected, and left in great numbers. Then, those who stayed were not able to do well in an unfamiliar industry, could not find the pride and sense of accomplishment and left, too.

At that time, the company faced troubles within and without. On the one hand, the internal staff was seriously drained, the remainders were unstable, and the company was no longer as strong as when it dealt in the electronic communication industry. On the other, when we just entered a brand-new industry, competitors and newcomers had sprung up. This great threat and unconventional tactical play had worsened our condition owing to our previous internal strategic change. At that time, I often wondered if this transformation was correct. Fortunately, time and practice finally gave me the best answer.

Now, the company is undergoing a second strategic transformation. In the future, our development focus will gradually be placed on the media industry, and we will get deep in it. Although this industrial transformation is so difficult and may even fail, I will continue to go on. Today, some employees are still concerned about their future work. Innovation is destined to be difficult. Every time, I comfort them with "It doesn't matter. We can explore together."

There is no end to innovation. Despite the present difficulty, which may even end in failure, it is impossible for a company to stop innovation for one day as long as it exists. Otherwise, the enterprise can only ruin itself. I believe that, with our joint efforts, it will be interesting and magnificent, and turn out to be another great spiritual wealth of Lanjiao Media despite hardships of every kind on the road to innovation. No matter what, we will be undaunted and courageous to start again and again.

Here, I am fully prepared to start another round of innovation together with all the Lanjiao people. The difference is that our team and mentality are more mature than the previous one, and I firmly believe that we can reverse the situation.

Tomorrow & Daring to Innovate

We are all familiar with the plight of ZTE.

In 2018, the US Department of Commerce issued a ban on export rights, prohibiting US companies from providing ZTE with all necessary parts, without which the company could hardly survive in the telecommunications industry. This shows the important role of technological innovation.

Innovation is the first driving force for development, and it is also the strategic support for building a socialist modern economic system. Our company, to go global, go big and go strong, must innovate independently. To be a truly strong country and achieve the goal of the great rejuvenation of the nation, China must take the road of innovation for strengthening itself.

For the enterprise itself, innovation is not only the improvement and replacement of the company's own products and technologies, but also the evolution of product concept and business cognition. Innovation is the key to business development.

As entrepreneurs who may have experienced some breakthroughs from the jungle of competition, we have a deep understanding of the power of innovation. Of course, innovation is a very broad topic, which covers technological innovation, and content innovation. Innovation for a company involves all aspects, not just simple product innovation, but also innovations such as corporate culture, corporate systems and industrial planning. Like our country, there are theoretical, institutional, technological and cultural innovations.

For the enterprise, the leadership must always keep the innovative thinking and the spirit of staying in step with the times, and always ask themselves as innovators, entrepreneurs, reformers and even revolutionaries.

For some time, I had been venturing in more than a dozen industries and looking for a path suitable for the development of my company by constantly "making revolution against myself." The road to innovation, like closing some trades, adjusting some strategy, re-layout, and promoting the company growth, is by no means easy, but only innovation is the key to the survival of an enterprise.

There is an extraordinary enterprise in any industry, but behind it is the courage of the company to be the first and to dare to innovate. B2C (business-to-guest) achievements Alibaba, sharing travel mode achievements Didi, Mobai, OFO, and countless stories about innovation, shine in the background of the times.

For enterprise development, innovation is the last straw at a critical moment. In 2019, Huawei got on the list of entities of the US Department of Commerce's Industry and Security Bureau. He Tingbo, president of Huawei's Haisi, said in a letter to his employees, "Even when all was thriving many years ago, the company made an assumption of extreme survival when all advanced chips and technologies in the United States would not be available one day, and Huawei will continue to serve customers. To prevent this from happening, thousands of Haisi people have embarked on the most tragic history in the history of science and technology. This Long March has created its 'backup tire' for survival." A decade of silent technological innovation, Huawei has not become another ZTE owing to the support of a strong technical strength from behind.

What is innovation?

Innovation is what we see today from the perspective of tomorrow. When you stand at a higher position and look at China now, from the perspective of the world, you will behave differently. In the past, I entered the digital industry and worked hard at a few inconspicuous desks. Although it was a traditional industry, the success behind it was due to the strategic importance of innovative thinking.

Accurately target your audience. Around 2010, we switched to the digital industry. Initially, we defined the consumer groups as college students in the second-and third-tier cities, especially freshmen. Their standard package is the mobile phone and computer, and purchase from a physical store was still popular then, so the potential market had plenty of room for traditional sales.

Advanced mode. For the market on the campus, the most important thing was to seize the students' purchase needs, and we recruited a large number of agents. If you were an agent, the people around you had a desire for purchase, so you had your customer(s). If you were a customer, during our return visit, you might be asked whether you wanted to act as an agent. Promotion after continuous understanding expanded the scope of customers.

Set the situation and solve problems. Each customer has his needs and each store its way of sales. From our non-stop simulation experiments, we have got the sales version fit for us. From understanding customer characteristics, such as demand, positioning, and potential price system, we set specific sales models, and constantly practiced them.

Differential Strategies. We have what others don't, and have something new they are short of. This is what we mean by differentiation. While we were doing digital, in addition to ordinary market products, we had to do products that others did not have. How did we rival Jingdong in the past? It was on the strategy of differentiation, in fact. For the price of the same product, we could lower a little as a physical store, together with an after-sales guarantee. Secondly, when the classic products were unavailable, we could sell exclusively.

A series of reactions could be brought along by innovative ideas and daring to try, and we had quickly grown into a leader in the digital plaza from an unknown store, and even become an unbeatable monument in the digital world. At that time, we had successfully downed our opponents and got the market as the only one throughout the Digital Square.

Regardless of the past or the future, no matter what field or project I choose, I am always the biggest pursuer of a model. Our innovation should be fixed on a field for deepening and studying, find out its pain point for treatment, then form a business model that conforms to the general trend and then continue to explore new models for innovation in this field.

In the future, we will involve ourselves in new projects, enter new environments, while maintaining the company's fine features. We will keep at our bold innovations, bold reforms, and even bold self-revolutions in accordance with new areas, new situations especially those overseas, and constantly innovate new management concepts, systems, and business models.

A business leader should heighten his ability to think independently, think more about the future direction of the industry, opportunities for future development of his company, problems to be faced, and the direction of future products and technical development. Under the premise of keeping cash flow, a leader must lead companies to try more innovations.

A company mustn't be rigid or cut off from its past system. We should continue to innovate whether to negate and affirm something.

On the path of brilliant China's innovation, our company must keep pace with the times. An enterprise should find its own position in the global chain of innovative industries, give full play to its advantages in its own field, and master the chain of the innovative industries by supplying what others are short of with our advantages, so as to further play our role in the entire industry. Finding its own position, keeping on, and constantly innovating, the enterprise will be invincible.

See the Future & Stick On

Seeing the future, we can take the next step. How to be sure of that? The test is on the height of thinking and the courage to predict the future.

The Book of Songs says something to this effect: While it is not raining yet, I must well strengthen the broken nest with the mulberry roots and skins.

In 1046 BC, King Wu of the Zhou Dynasty destroyed the Shang Dynasty. To appease its people, he made Prince Wugeng a duke of Chaoke. In praise of the military deeds against Shang, Lords Zhou, Tai, Zhao and others were retained in the Capital City to aid King Wu, of whom Lord Zhou was most trusted.

Two years later, King Wu got seriously ill. Lord Zhou expressed his willingness to die instead of his elder brother while attending sacrificial church to his ancestors, wishing the King a speedy recovery. After that, he sealed his wish in a stone room, strictly forbidding any leakage by the history recording officials.

The next day, King Wu's health turned for the better, but soon relapsed and eventually died. The young Prince Jisong was crowned, called King Cheng in history, and Lord Zhou was made the regent by King Wu in a will.

However, his regency caused dissatisfaction with Guan Shu and others, who spread rumors that he was meant for usurping the throne. These rumors triggered the new king's suspicion, and the regent had no choice but to leave the Capital.

Seeing this discord between the uncle and nephew, Lord Wu Geng immediately sent for Guan Shu and others to worsen their relationship with Lord Zhou while actively preparing for an armed rebellion.

After he left, Lord Zhou's careful planning had finally assured the source of rumors and learned about the evil intent Lord Wu Geng and his ilk had harbored. He anxiously wrote a poem entitled "Chixiao (a fierce bird resembling an owl)" to King Cheng, expressing his deep concern about the state affairs in the tone of the mother bird.

However, the young king failed to learn what Lord Zhou really meant and stayed indifferent. Later, happening to find Lord Zhou's message in the stone room, the king was deeply touched. He immediately sent for Lord Zhou. Back in the Capital, King Cheng had him lead troops to conquer Guan Shu and Lord Wu Geng. Lord Zhou's resourcefulness quickly had the rebellion quelled, and the rule of the Zhou Dynasty was further consolidated.

Imagine that, without Lord Zhou's foresight, the Zhou Dynasty could never have seen its prosperity and stability. In the Ming Dynasty, there was a sentence in *Zhu Family Instructions* that "better get ready before the rain and dig the well before you are thirsty." This later became the popular expression of "preparedness against the rainy day". This ancient idiom still carries its light of eye-catching wisdom in modern society. The daring to judge the future market is a strategic height.

We have explored in more than a dozen industries, constantly rejecting our choices, and finally found the media suitable for our future direction. In the future, Lanjiao Media will go to the world and let the world listen to the voice of China. It is also an attempt to predict the future for the rainy day.

Propelled by the national strategic level, various "mass innovation spaces" and "industrial parks" have been spreading rapidly, as if there has come the trend of "incubating China". Entrepreneurship is not quite often based on what projects you prefer, for the reality must first considered. Someone asked why we chose to follow the digital industry? In fact, it was mostly for survival. Nowadays, Lanjiao Media will be our lifelong undertaking. We are committed to making it a leader of the industry and let the world turn their eyes to China's media. We also believe that culture can break all barriers.

Culture is an important force for the survival and development of the nation. Chinese culture has a long history of 5,000 years. From ancient times to the present, it has given the Chinese people a constant strength. We, born in this great era, should strengthen our cultural self-confidence, and follow the report to the 19th CPC National Congress, which brought forth the concept of "promoting the creative transformation of Chinese outstanding traditional culture and innovative development, inheriting revolutionary culture, developing advanced socialist culture, bearing in mind our aspiration, absorbing what is foreign and being future-oriented", and promote Chinese culture to the outside world.

Undoubtedly, when material civilization has developed to a certain height, spiritual civilization will definitely play a leading role. Combining the background of the times with its own dream, Lanjiao Media will firmly develop its cultural industry in the future.

Only by focusing on clear positioning in combination with the advantages of the company for business and deep research can it possibly come out first in the industry. When doing an industry, you have to be in it.

To see the future, the premise is to follow the national development policy. We are in this era when the country needs cultural development, and the people need high-quality cultural content. For entrepreneurs, this is our great opportunity, and bringing about a new glory of Chinese culture is the mission to each of us in the cultural industry.

Today, under the guidance of building a strong socialist cultural country, our company must adhere to the concept of serving the people and socialism and insist on spreading the positive energy to society.

With the company development and the individual growth and maturity, we should be clearer that culture is a powerful spiritual force. In the future, Lanjiao Media will strive to create cultural output of positive energy, focusing on publications such as short videos for positive energy and comprehensive culture, so as to well disseminate Chinese traditional culture, Chinese stories and Asian civilization.

China needs an industry for cultural creation and spiritual civilization. We are fortunate to find such a point of convergence between the times and entrepreneurship. Lanjiao Media is what our hearts are after, which not only extends our childhood dream, but also plays a role in making Chinese culture go global.

As the country vigorously promotes the development of modern cultural industries, we must all the more respond to the call of the times. In the past, we have been looking for a cause that benefits the country and the people and carries a feeling of patriotism. Now that we have found it, what reason do we have not to invest in and support it?

Seeing the future means being unafraid of competition. The competition for the media industry is very fierce in Sichuan, let alone across the country because of such enterprises as light, Huayi and various media groups, but Lanjiao Media has never been afraid of competition from the bottom of its heart.

We have always regarded competition as a good thing. We are not afraid of it. We have experienced many failures, so what if there is one more? I believe that failure is the mother of success. Being small now does not mean so in the future. From the Blue Sea at the start-up to the Red Sea, we have always been able to adapt to new markets. After leaving the crowded Red Sea market, we have the ability to enter a huge blue sea market for a rapid growth. The former Huawei, compared with Ericsson and Siemens, could not be so eye-catching. But now, its 5G has left the competitors behind.

After all, the times will not disappoint those who work hard. We have identified the direction of the cultural industry and have recognized that our personal mission and cultural dream are closely linked to the destiny of the country and the nation, so we will forge ahead against difficulties, however tense the competition or whether we will fail 100 times.

Look toward the future with no fear of competition, keep our aspiration at heart, and march on. We will always pay close attention to what we want and what our mission and strategy are. Only from the competition can we find and make up for our shortage. Only competition can make us work harder.

Seeing the future need our adherence all the more to the entrepreneurial spirit. We must have a global structure, do global business, get global partners, and welcome people from all over the world for investment. However, we must never forget our Chinese root. Inheriting and carrying forward the past entrepreneurs' strong national sentiment, we must stand firm when it comes to national justice and interests.

I once said that if my company in the US or some overseas platform needs me to emigrate in the future, I would rather turn off that platform and make less money than lose my Chinese nationality.

In the future, I will devote myself to China, Asia, and the world. But at a crucial time, none of my choice, my national sentiment, and justice for my country must be lost.

Seeing the future and sticking to the road ahead, we contemporary entrepreneurs and youth must shoulder our responsibilities for the nation. At a critical moment, we must remember that we are Chinese, resist all temptations in life choices and keep virtuea even at the cost of great interests.

China's Road & Innovation

"Innovate or die." The earth is in constant motion. Every day, countless new things and ideas keep coming forth into the world while countless others are eliminated.

"How is water so bright and clear? Just fresh from its source down here." If there is no fresh water from the source, the water in the rivers and lakes will soon become a turbid, lifeless and stagnant. In the same way, without the consciousness and spirit of constant innovation, a country and a nation will lose its hope of development, and a company its foundation and a person his motivation to move forward.

In the long history, with the continuous innovations in the political system, agriculture, handicrafts, commerce, ideology and culture, science and technology, the Chinese nation has maintained its leading position in the world. In 2007, among the 101 inventions that had changed the world selected The Independent, a British newspaper, the four major inventions of papermaking, printing, compass, gunpowder as well as the abacus in ancient China were on the list.

According to historians and economists, China's per capita GDP was $ 450 based on the 1990 benchmark rate after the Song Dynasty was established, and it was $600 when it ended. In the same period of European society at the Middle Ages, the figure was $422. The famous British economic historian Madison once wrote, "As early as the 10th century, China's per capita income was already the leader in the world economy, and this lasted until the 15th century. On the technical level, China's tapping and utilization of resources and management of its vast territory have surpassed Europe."

So, what caused its subsequent decline? The reasons are very complicated. Various opinions exist in the field of history. But to my way of thinking, being content with the present state instead of innovation must be one of them.

"China has completely fallen behind the West right from the prime of the Qianlong's reign". In 1793, as the feudal society almost came to an end, Emperor Qianlong flatly rejected the British delegation's request for trade. In his letter to the King of England, he still used the tone of a heavenly kingdom to the effect as follows, "I have perused your memorial: the earnest terms in which it is couched reveal a respectful humility on your part, which is highly praiseworthy... Moreover, our Celestial dynasty possesses vast territories, and tribute missions from the dependencies are provided for by the Department for Tributary States..." Little did Qianlong know that the Qing Dynasty at that time was far behind the advanced countries of the world such as Great Britain.

It is nothing terrible to be behind for some time, but what is so horrible is that people have no sense of innovation and change. Under the political background of feudal autocracy, top-down reform and innovation cannot touch the soft spot, and no success can come. When the Qing Dynasty was over, countless people with lofty ideals rushed up and down, and promoted reform and innovation from all aspects such as political system, economic development, ideology and culture, and actively explored the development path that conformed to China's national conditions and reality.

Since the founding of New China, according to the special national conditions, the Chinese people have implemented various epoch-making great innovations from the theoretical line, political system, and economic system, and gradually found out the socialist development path with Chinese characteristics.

On the theoretical level, we have Marxism, MAO Zedong Thought, Deng Xiaoping Theory, the important thought of Three Represents, the Scientific Outlook on Development and Xi Jinping Thought on Socialism with Chinese Characteristics for the New Era. On the political level, we have created advanced systems such as the "People's Congress System", "Political Consultation Conference System", "National Regional Autonomy System" and "One Country, Two Systems".

On the economic level, we have carried out measures such as "Three Major Socialist Transformations", "Fixing Farm Output Quotas for Each Household" and "Reform and Opening up."

Through various innovations, China has undergone earth-shaking changes in just a few decades, and its overall national strength has been increasing.

Nowadays, with China's increase in economic strength, Chinese culture has also begun to go global and it has become a major country with world influence. We are in the key historical node of the great rejuvenation of the Chinese nation and the restart of reform and opening up, so we must place innovation in an important position.

Specifically, in terms of theoretical innovation, we must "complete and develop the socialist system with Chinese characteristics, advance the national governance system and the governance capacity as the general goal for comprehensively deepening the reform, and bravely promote theoretical, practical, institutional innovations and others. Innovate in all aspects, continue to advance with the times and promote the continuous development of Marxism." [1]

In terms of technological innovation, we must vigorously develop sci-tech and promote China's sci-tech to become the innovation highland of the world science center, constantly put sci-tech innovation in a more important and prominent position and take the road of science to strengthen the country. With the continuous progress of the times, we must firmly hold the major sci-tech achievements in our own hands and persist in self-reliance and independent innovation.

In terms of cultural innovation, we must "dare to innovate and create, promote the development of cultural innovation with exquisite art" and "explore deep into the ideological concepts, humanistic spirit, and moral norms contained in the fine traditional culture of China, and inherit the innovations as the era requires, so that Chinese culture can display its permanent charm and image of the times." [2]

Talent is an important foundation for innovation and a key factor in driving innovation. We often say that innovation is actually driven by talent. In terms of talent innovation, we must build a globally competitive talent system, break down barriers of systems and mechanisms, gather talent from all over the world, loosen what binds

---

[1] Bao Xinjian,"Improve and develop Socialist System with Chinese Characteristics in Reform and Opening up", *Guangming Daily*, 24 December, 2018.

[2] Xu Guangyou,"VigorouslyInherit and Promote Chinese Excellent Traditional Culture", *Learning Times*, 17 April, 2019.

them, and release their vitality of innovation and creativity, so that they can develop their strengths.

Innovation is a booster for the development of the country and the enterprise. Today, both individuals and enterprises are going all out for innovation. I am sure that our motherland will embark on a brilliant road to innovation.

Part IV

Major Country for Globalized Era of 4.0

“ **A single flower does not make spring, while one hundred flowers in full blossom bring spring to the garden.**

Ancient and Present Aphorisms ”

Through a series of maritime activities in the 15th century, navigators of West Europe opened up new routes with slavery, violence and commerce, enabling the world to move toward unity. This is the era of globalization 1.0.

Later, owing to such a series of events as the industrial revolution, capitalist political reform, and imperialist colonization, the world began to enter the era of globalization 2.0 dominated by the United Kingdom.

After World War II came the era of globalization 3.0 led by the United States. After the 2008 financial crisis, with the changes in international politics, economy, culture and many other patterns, the system of globalization entered a critical period of fission.

Currently, the world is entering the era of globalization 4.0 on the basis of the fourth industrial revolution. For China, this is both an opportunity and a challenge. The opportunity is that China can use this world to promote its development in all aspects; the challenge is that there are still many obstacles in the current world that are not conducive to the process of globalization.

Globalization is the unstoppable trend of the times. Now, we live in a global village with all the other countries, where Chinese brands such as Huawei and Haier can be seen abroad. China's new four inventions of high-speed rail, scan code payment, shared bicycle and online shopping have gradually entered the world, which has greatly influenced the people's life of across the world.

At this historical stage, the Chinese youth must have the right vision and mind fit for a major country, care about international events, human destiny and globalization, and view problems and do things from a global perspective.

10 Start of New Era

The contemporary youth are in a good era whether for the world or China.

Now, the process of globalization has reached a new historical stage in which China plays a very important role.

How to live up to the good times? The only answer is "struggle". As the Chinese youth, we must base ourselves on our country, go to the world, and make necessary contributions to the motherland and the world.

New Commercial Civilization

This is the best time when everyone has the opportunity to start his business and realize his dream. The country has given us entrepreneurial advantages different from the past. Technology has enabled information to spread fast and far. Time and space are no longer the state of slow horses and insurmountable mountains, and the world has narrowed itself into a global village, where people have almost no sense of distance.

The new commercial civilization has long been with us. Gone is the past old style, which only focused on maximizing profits and shareholders' rights. In this leaf of an ark of the world, the concept of openness, transparency, sharing, and responsibility has become the trend of the times.

What is the new commercial civilization?

In fact, it is what different people view the same thing. All in all, in such an era, enterprises only need to do two things: do your things and mind others. The former requires that you do what you need and be responsible for your enterprise and the latter demands that you stay clear about the relationship between business development and society.

As an entrepreneur who has influenced the nation, Chu Shijian has practiced these two things all his life, so to speak. During his 18 years' dedication to Hongtashan Tobacco Factory, Chu had turned it from the dying moment into "a flag for Chinese national enterprises" by creating a huge amount of profit and tax for the country.

He used to say, "While running an enterprise, we must first consider how much it impacts and how good it is for the country." When seen today, this is the core concept of the new commercial civilization.

Today in the 21st century, the new commercial civilization pursues the core concept of openness, transparency, sharing and responsibility. Openness is the soul of its innovation; transparency is its starting point; sharing is the driving force behind its formation and proliferation; and responsibility is its constant and inseparable part.

Under the influence of the new commercial civilization, an enterprise no longer limits itself to profit, but constantly leans toward responsibility. For entrepreneurs under the new commercial civilization, our mission is to assume more social responsibilities by following the tide and progress of the times.

Profitability is the important prerequisite for the sustainable development of an enterprise, and the material basis responsible for employees. This is the common feature either for the old or new commercial civilization. As entrepreneurs, we should first consider how to promote the long-term operation and development of our enterprises. "Before your success, strive for self-cultivation; when in success, try to serve the world." If the company can't guarantee its own survival and development, and grow big and strong, then what responsibility can it have to offer?

At the same time, entrepreneurs are face to face with two major changes.

The first is the transformation from the material level of pursuing interests to the spiritual level of responsibility. In the process of enterprise development, responsibility should never be ignored. Only when an enterprise has its culture and mission, and creates values for the society, can it survive and develop in a healthy way.

No enterprise can separate itself from the times, much less from the country. It should forge ahead with opportunity for development while actively taking its social responsibility under the national policy.

As is known to everyone, the rise of Shanxi merchants owed a lot to the Kaizhong Salt Law in the Ming Dynasty. But that was a time when the border was fraught with war and strife. When life and property were at risk, these merchants knew all the more that protecting the country meant protecting the families.

The Shanxi merchants had great difficulty transporting grain and iron around the fortresses only to be more often than not looted and plundered. Countless people had lost their lives in a strange land. However, they knew that only when the country was peaceful could their small families stay stable.

Today, we are far from war, yet in ancient times, the social responsibility and love of the country shown by the Shanxi merchants were by no means obsolete. Isn't this the spirit of entrepreneurship, as is seen now?

We all know that the best embodiment of entrepreneurship is social responsibility. In the era of new commercial civilization, more entrepreneurs have begun to form a sense of responsibility on the spiritual level. For social development, this is an extremely powerful driving force.

Second, the transformation from “small self” to “great self”. And its shift of focus moves from the individual and enterprise to the society and country, and even to the world.This very broadly shows the increase of the vision on the part of an entrepreneur. While following the times, Chinese entrepreneurs have to re-examine themselves and find their own positions. While the enterprise is developing steadily, we must know how to repay the society.

Peter F. Drucker once mentioned, “The most fundamental reason for the continuous prosperity of the US economy to even exceed most economists’ predictions of its economic cycle is the emergence of a real entrepreneurial economy. This is the most far-reaching and inspiring thing in economic history.”

In the same way, we have every reason to believe that what China’s reform and opening up for more than 40 years has achieved can hardly be separated from the promotion of entrepreneurs from behind. In the era of new commercial civilization, entrepreneurs have been shouldering the mission for promoting the prosperity and development of the motherland and realizing the great rejuvenation of the Chinese nation, and they should be even more active in shouldering social responsibilities and creating social values.

Not a few entrepreneurs had explored the new commercial civilization in the first decade of the 21st century. In my early 20s, I was still struggling from one traditional industry to another but was no stranger to the civilization mentioned. Now, in our 13th year of entrepreneurship, our understanding of our society and career has gradually matured. Targeted poverty alleviation and self-improvement scholarships in high schools are all our attempts as part of social responsibility.

Under the new commercial civilization, responsibility is no longer limited to one enterprise only, but to the entire society instead. Starting a company is no longer purely making profits. Charity, social responsibility, and win-win cooperation have become important indicators for sharpening an enterprise's competitiveness.

The measure for the success of an enterprise is not just the amount of profit, but the social values it creates. An enterprise must not only provide a good platform for the mutual growth of its employees and partners but also give them the opportunity for realizing their values in life. Only when an enterprise enables its staff to bravely pursue their dreams and realize their material and spiritual needs can it continue to develop for a longer period of time.

While addressing the appeals of our employees and partners, we must see those of the state and society and make corresponding contributions to them. This responsibility is the mission of us entrepreneurs as well as my own understanding of the new commercial civilization.

Chen Chunhua, a famous Chinese corporate culture and strategy expert, once said, "I admire entrepreneurs so much not for their great wealth, but their ability to actually turn a concept into a real reality and produce real value. I think this is the most powerful part of entrepreneurship, which is of great importance to our society."

Entrepreneurs turn their ideas into reality and blueprints into high-rises. This spirit of boldness to be the first and to dream is not only what our society also we contemporary youth need.

The new business civilization gives us more opportunities, and everyone's future is based on the present, so the best way for us to embrace the future is to excel in what we are doing right now.

Globalization

In today's world, globalization is an irresistible trend. In his book *The World Is Flat*, Thomas Friedman described such a scene, "When I was a child, my parents used to say: My son, be good and finish the meal because the children in China and India have nothing to eat. But now, the parents say: Be a good girl and finish your college, because the children in China and India are waiting to take the bread out of your mouth."

Regardless of whether it agrees or not with the children of the above countries, what can be ascertained is that globalization, while creating opportunities and convenience for people around the world, inevitably brings new challenges and problems.

Now, around the world, some voices against globalization are getting sharper. In my opinion, this way of giving up innovations is far from desirable. As Friedman said, "When the world becomes flat and you feel this pressure, you should tap your potentials for the challenge, but not build protective walls of every kind."

In the mid-19th century, when the world began to reunite, a British economist had the following paragraph, "Oceania has our sheep farms, and our cattle in the western grasslands of Argentina and North America... Peru has sent its silver, South Africa and Australia's gold has flown to London, the Indians and Chinese have been growing tea for us, while our coffee, sugar and spice plantations have been spread across the East Indies..."

If globalization, since its very beginning and for a long time after, has carried a great color of the strong plundering the weak, and now, it functions more as a creator for a better and more harmonious life for all mankind by profoundly practicing the theme of the times of peace and development. Despite occasional conflicts and confrontations between countries, consultations and dialogues are becoming the mainstream in place of war and might of the big powers.

The enterprise is an indispensable force in the process of globalization.

Huawei is a typical global company, and it has been one from the very beginning. In this regard, Ren Zhengfei once bluntly said, "Huawei is not a local Chinese company. It has gathered the strength after plenty of struggle before going 'global' and developing its colonies across the world. Our products have never been produced 'independently'. Huawei is a global company and, since the very beginning, we have integrated global resources, produced the best products, served the people around the world, and created value for human beings."

According to one of its former employees, Huawei's largest software team is in India at this stage, its Aesthetics Institute in France, and its algorithmic elite mainly concentrated in Moscow, and the Institute in Japan is mainly responsible for the techniques of some devices and material.

It must be said that Huawei mobile phones have been manufactured through the joint development of the global powers. From R &D and manufacturing to logistics and sales, it has been integrating the world's best resources to create the highest quality products for the world. Nowadays, most people around the world can easily get such a mobile phone. This is Huawei's vision of globalization. We can say with certainty that any company today hoping to make a difference must establish a close relationship with the world.

On February 13, 2019, Lanjiao Media Co., Ltd., a wholly owned subsidiary of our company in Las Vegas, USA, was officially established. The company has offices in New York, Illinois, and Delaware, and its business covers investment, finance, and cultural industries. It is an important foundation for Lanjiao Media to build a strategic development platform in North America, and also an important strategic step of mine to implement overseas development.

In addition, Asia Civilization Culture Media Co., Ltd. will dedicate itself to positive energy short video, comprehensive cultural publishing and other businesses, disseminate excellent Chinese traditional culture, Chinese stories and Asian Civilization, and strive to the one for the inheritance and protection of Asian Civilization and the humanist builder for the community of common destiny for mankind.

Meanwhile, we will get deeply involved in the process of globalization, deploying corresponding cultural industries around the world, integrating the valuable cultural resources of all countries and nations, discovering outstanding cultural talent from all over the world, and competing and cooperating with cultural enterprises from all over the world...

In December 2018, the Global Think Tank (CCG), together with Finance & Economics Development Institute, Southwestern University and Social Science Literature Publishing House, released the Blueprint for Corporate Internationalization in *China Business Globalization Report (2018)*.

The report shows that the rising tide worldwide against globalization is the main reason for the decline of global foreign direct investment in 2017. For example, in the US, the Trump administration implemented trade protectionism, bringing about an abrupt increase of uncertainty in global trade and international economic cooperation. In Europe, the elections of some important countries such as Germany and France reflected the expansion of European right-wing forces, which might become an important factor hindering the development of globalization. In addition, the US and European investment protectionism tends to be strengthened through the formulation or revision of laws for strengthening foreign investment review system and providing a legal basis for the government to review foreign M&A."

It can be foreseen that the future globalization may be full of twists and turns. Despite all kinds of uncertainties and unfriendly factors, I believe that the situation can always be stronger than people. Since ancient times, the general trend has been unstoppable. For example, Dr. Sun Yat-sen once said that "So great is the world tide that one prospers by following it and perishes by going against it."

Numerous elements such as capital, technology, culture, talent, and resources have been shuttling through the world in order to find their best positions. As a global company, we will also plunge ourselves in this wave, so as to gather the power of the world to do some real good things for the country and for all mankind.

China Today as One of the World

From ancient times to the present, after a tumultuous development process, the Asian people have jointly created brilliant achievements in civilization. At a time when cultural exchanges and mutual learning are becoming more frequent, they are so eager to jointly establish an Asia that is peaceful, harmonious, and prosperous.

Asia has all along been a big family. It may have had arguments and disputes in the past. But today, in the context of peace and development as the subject matter of the world, the exchange of civilizations is the main theme of the common development of Asian countries. Our culture, religion, and ideology have a lot in common. Our geographical location decides that we are close neighbors connected by mountains and rivers as a whole.

Every civilization is a continuation of the blood of the country and the nation. Asian civilization, so rich and colorful, requires to be passed on from one generation to another by us contemporary youth by stay in step with the times. The diversity of Asian civilization requires that we not only recognize our own, but also appreciate that of others.

What role should China play in it?

I think that the following paragraph by General Secretary Xi Jinping is so to the point. "China today is not only China itself, but also that in Asia and in the world; China will embrace the world in the future with a more open attitude and contribute to the world with its more vigorous achievements of civilization." [1]

How should the young people, as a generation in between, undertake the mission and bring the Chinese civilization to the world? How to tell the Chinese story on the world stage?

At the parallel sub-forum of the Asian Civilization Dialogue Conference, my friend Liao Yujing mentioned that Huo Qigang, vice president of Huo Yingdong

---

[1] Xi Jinping,"Provide a Way for the World People to Explore the Road to Development", *People's Daily*, 19 May, 2019.

Group, had left him the most impressive memory. Huo believes that it is a prerequisite to engage in a dialogue of civilizations. That is to say, while understanding your own, you must recognize that of others. At 12, He went to the UK alone. In that culturally unfamiliar environment, he did everything he could for understanding and tolerance.

Exchanges and mutual learning make civilizations richer and more colorful. Today's China faces the world with a more open and inclusive attitude and contributes to it with more energetic achievements. At this important historical node of exchange and mutual understanding of Asian civilization, and the historic moment of development for human civilization, we young Chinese deeply feel on us the great responsibility and the glory of the mission.

On the one hand, we must respond to General Secretary Xi Jinping's call in his keynote speech at the opening ceremony of Asian Civilization Dialogue Conference, promote exchanges and mutual learning between different countries, nationalities and cultures around the world, consolidate the humanistic foundation of the community of common destiny for Asia and that of common destiny for mankind and create a series of "Chinese Youth Name cards", leading the inheritance of Asian civilization with our youthful strength.

Now, both I and Liao Yujing, "one of the most promising young writers in China" (commented by the British *Financial Times*) actively respond to the launch China Colorful Civilization Development Foundation, and strive as its inheritors and champions to create a beautiful future for Asian and world civilizations.

Youth is the future of the nation and the hope of the country. It is also a powerful force for strengthening and inheriting the connection and communication of

Asian civilization. As contemporary Chinese youth, we must understand and follow the general trend, be oriented to the future, deepen our understanding of the differences between Chinese civilization and other cultures, and promote their exchanges and dialogues. We must bear the responsibility and mission bestowed on us by the times, strive to be the inheritors and champions of Asian civilization and the holders of the "Chinese Youth Name Card", so as to create a new Asia through mutual learning and inspiration and bring it to a new peak through inheritance and development.

The building of socialism with Chinese characteristics has entered a new historical stage, so the younger generation should assume the sacred mission of recording, writ- ing and eulogizing this new era as soon as possible.

The historical change and cultural map of this era need to be recorded by our generation. The great rejuvenation of the Chinese nation requires not only the progress of material civilization, but also that of spiritual civilization. The building of socialist cultural civilization is an important cause of the Party and the country, and an important source of strength for the nation and the people.

Relying on the high regard of the Party and the country for literary and artistic works and cultural undertakings, as a holder of the "China Youth Name Card", I have set up a media limited liability company meant for the creation of positive energy videos and literary works.

The present generation has grown up in a fast-selling culture. In the past, the Chinese youth tried to break away with what limited them for the spread of vernacular Chinese. They had the great ambitions for the rise of China and for studying overseas for serving the motherland. Today, we are faced with a more complex world than any other era: Information explosion, clashes of ideas, and rapid development of the Internet. If we are a little mentally slack, what may dominate is still Western culture, or a fast-selling culture devoid of connotation.

Under such a background, the inevitable choice for realizing the great rejuvenation of the Chinese nation is to strengthen cultural self-confidence.

We the youth are where social vitality lies. We can quickly accept new knowledge and new technologies. We should take on more responsibilities for inheriting and carrying forward traditional culture by embracing strong patriotism and writing the main theme of the times.

Now, the short videos represented by Tik Tok have become a popular trend among the youth. We have started Asian Civilization Culture Media Co., Ltd., so as to put out positive energy culture and deliver high quality contents. The cultural industry is duty- bound for those in the cultural industry to inspire the national spirit with literature and art and establish national self-confidence with culture.

We must not only inherit Chinese traditional culture, but also make sure of the pulse of the times, bear its mission, and listen to its voice. We should offer proper authoritative interpretation and transmission by various means. We must constantly promote the artistic innovation, enhance the quality of literary and artistic works, walk in step with the broad masses and create the literary and artistic works popular with the public.

As Chinese youth with aspirations and ideals, we must not only leave some memory for the times but also publicize the energy for the present.

In the future setup of any new company, I will continue to advocate values for positive energy, conform to the requirement and call of the times, be an inheritor and champion of Asian civilization, a humanistic builder of the community of common destiny for Asia and that of common destiny for mankind. It is the mission and responsibility of us contemporary youth to convey the positive energy to the society, transmit our voice, and laud the healthy and progressive attitude of life with positive cultural works.

I believe that, as a response to the call of the Party and the government, either China Colorful Civilization Development Foundation under preparation, or the cultural transmission company to be established can be of help for the Chinese youth to go global and propel the Asian people to further understand each other so that different cultural forms can deepen their exchanges and learn from each other, highlight the rich and enduring vitality of Asian culture, and deepen the development appeal for the community of common destiny for Asia and that of common destiny for all mankind.

Go Global & Be Rooted in China

Huawei in Chinese means a lot: Go global but be rooted in China.

Since its establishment in Shenzhen, Guangdong in 1987, Huawei has been constantly building its business landscape on a global scale. According to its 2018 annual report, Huawei had a total of 188,000 employees and operated in more than 170 countries and regions, serving more than a population of 3 billion.

In its 5G technology business segment, Huawei has obtained more than 30 contracts of 5G worldwide with a coverage of customers in Europe, Middle East and Asia Pacific. The cumulative shipment of 45,000 5G base stations has been sent globally. With more than 10,000 sets of base stations, its share in China on solid footing.

It is a global company, but, first of all, a national enterprise rooted in China. This is evident from the name of its new system. Some time ago, it announced the name of the newly developed own operating system – "Hong Meng", the literary meaning of which is "a chaotic spirit before the opening of heaven and earth". According to Chinese mythology, before Pangu created the whole world in ancient times in the Kunlun Mountains, it was a chaotic spirit, and this natural vitality was thus called and referred often later on to ancient times. In Dream of Red Mansions, there is a sentence of "Ever since long ago, who has stayed so sentimental? Just for that very love."

In combination with Huawei's current situation, it not only represents the enterprise's determination to start from scratch, but also shows the world its great national complex. In addition, Huawei has registered quite some good names in Chinese. Its mobile phone chip is called "Kylin or Chinese unicorn", baseband chip "Baron or dragon", server chip "Roc", and server platform "Taishan or Mt Tai", router chip "Lingxiao or the sky", and artificial intelligence chip "Shengteng or Rise".

In May 2019, when being interviewed on CCTV's "One on One", Ren Zhengfei made clear Huawei people's great patriotic heart, "We love our country, hope to see it prosperous and strong, and won't be bullied again."

A global enterprise, no matter how strong it gets, must never forget where its root is. In my opinion, this very sentence has two levels of meaning. First, while the company shines on the world stage, it must continue to be grateful to and support its own country and, to a certain extent, retain and convey to the world its spiritual culture and values. Second, the motherland and its people, which is always the strong backing and will first reach out their hands to the enterprise when the enterprise is in difficulty.

"The son of a Chinese farmer who went from the fields to the world", is a description of the founder Lu Guanqiu on the official website of Wanxiang Group. In the book *Lu Guanqiu: Gathering Strength for the Universe*, Wanxiang's road to entrepreneurship is divided into five major stages. Among them, the last two are "Global Innovation (2011-2015): From the Fields to the World" and "Ecological Entrepreneurship (2015—): Return the Fields from the World."

While striding into the world, Wanxiang Group has never forgot its root and birthplace. In 1969, Wanxiang started from a simple small plant for agricultural machinery in Xiaoshan, Hangzhou. Few decades later, when it had grown into a modern multinational group with a revenue of over ¥ 100 billion and involved itself in such industries as agriculture, finance, and new energy, Wanxiang returned to Xiaoshan and started the construction project of the innovative energy city.

Lu Guanqiu's grand plan described that this is "Wanxiang Innovation Energy City which can gather not only electricity and talent, but also skill and technology, and which can be truly influential in the world, and well-placed at home."

After he died of illness, and his son Lu Weiding took his place. "In the future, people don't have to envy Silicon Valley. The future of Innovation Energy City will be as such and produce a team of entrepreneurial projects so influential in the world. We hope to create more works that can last forever. It is an opportunity for future development." Should what is said in the paragraph above become a reality, the wealth and development opportunities to Xiaoshan by Wanxiang Group will see no end.

In the future, our new company will follow the model roles of Huawei and Wanxiang with our aspiration and mission at heart. At the same time when the bugle of the times has been sounded to go global, the company will take on the heavy responsibility bestowed by the new era and continue to do what we can as our thanks to the country and society.

Chengdu, of Sichuan, will be our home base. In the past, Lanjiao Media radiated little by little from the communities and schools around and insisted on doing public welfare. In the future, we will continue to uphold this principle, radiating from the New and High-tech Area to Sichuan, China and the rest world. Of course, as a native company of Chengdu, Lanjiao Media will definitely invest more resources in the construction and support there.

"Gratitude for whatever little help". In the past seven years, if we had no markets, customers or resources provided by Sichuan, we wouldn't have been so developed as we are today, let alone go out of China for a far greater world. Therefore, when we achieve a grander dream on the world stage, we will never forget our kind-hearted Sichuan people.

we will in the future lay out and develop cultural undertakings all over the world, spare no effort to tell the world the Chinese stories, spread the Chinese voice, and display Chinese image with whatever bit we have for realizing the Chinese Dream.

Go global and be rooted in China. In my vision, Asian Civilization Culture Media Co., Ltd. has the soul of the Chinese nation, and can externally bring resources from all over the world to their own use.

Cultural Strength & Long History

The wheel of history keeps going forward, and many past things have been crushed into pieces except for its everlasting culture, which has an endless power for survival in the world. Despite the passage of history, we can still perceive the ideological spirit of Confucius and the philosophical implication of Socrates.

We have harvested the wisdom of our predecessors while moving forward with the times. But what can our generation leave for our successors?

This is an issue so practical. On some simple thinking, one can realize that all physical things will disappear one day in smoke, whether it is a house or a bridge, but the real culture that has withstood the test of time is always the ideology and culture devoid of the physical carrier. As a simple example shows, Disney, as one of such cultural companies, has brought countless people a sentiment because it has accompanied their growth.

Disney, far more than an animated film industry, involves theme parks, toys, books, clothing, accessories, bags, furniture and so on. Despite its span across various industries, Disney is still well received by consumers because of its cultural influence.

Mickey Mouse is the most typical representative. On November 18, 1928, with the release of the world's first cartoon movie "Steamboat Willie", Mickey Mouse swept the whole United States and even the rest world. In the 1980s, it came to China in the wake of its reform and opening up, and still owns a large number of fans. This show how penetrating the power of culture can be.

What of our time can we leave to our future generation? I think, nothing but culture. Isn't it the sorrow of the Chinese cultural industry if the younger generation recalls the box office films far ahead in the movie market but what first comes to their mind is Hollywood?This does not mean that China has no fine films, but it needs more such as “War Wolf”, “Mekong Action” and “I am no drug god”.

Now, I am writing this book, and will create a series of books and works, all aimed at spreading the mainstream values and positive energy culture, promoting exchanges and mutual learning between different countries, different nationalities and different cultures throughout the world, thus building to the best of my ability the community of common destiny for Asia and that of common destiny for mankind.

As the power of culture is sustainable, the determined development for the cultural industry requires that we lead the fashion of the times with noble cultural works. In the future, I will commit myself to its development, focusing on the field of children and women while delivering positive energy to society.

Young children, like saplings, are the hope of the motherland. Since the 18th CPC National Congress, the Party Central Committee with General Secretary Xi Jinping at the core has stood at the strategic height of guaranteeing the success to the national cause, closely heeding the growth of adolescents and children.

As contemporary young entrepreneurs, we are to carry the great mission and responsibility of the new era. I believe that only by integrating the ideal of life into the great cause of the nation can individuals achieve something. Education concerns the country, the nation, and the future. Children’s education is an important guarantee for laying a foundation for their life.

To this end, the new company may also promote the healthy growth of adolescents and children in the future and help the education of their development. When

I donated the High School affiliated to Southwest Jiaotong University in 2017, I mentioned my feedback to education just for the future of more children. Since then, I have also been encouraging the employees to return to school to donate and set up scholarship programs to help more local children to achieve better growth through education.

Every step for the journey of life is crucial. One step amiss disturbs every one after. And education plays a pivotal role in it. As a post-80s entrepreneur, I had plenty of hardships concerning schooling and entrepreneurship. It is because of all this that I hope to contribute my energy to their education.

In addition to supporting their education through donations, we may focus our efforts on audio and video products, film and television literature for their development, so as to foster their positive and optimistic attitude in life. Personality determines fate. What a person says or does when young will have a profound impact on his life.

Without the liberation and progress of women, there will be no liberation and progress of the entire human race. Based on this, we will focus on protecting women's rights and interests, creating cultural works that give full play to their positive energy, and supporting them to make contributions and realize their values.

For their development of careers, an enterprise must first respect the status of its female employees. All along, our company has been carrying forward the fine tradition for respecting and protecting women while they create wealth for the company as best as they can.

For developing their cultural undertakings, our company must join hands with the Women's Federation, listen carefully to their voices, truly reflect their voices, and do practical things for them. As a young entrepreneur, I will use my cultural transmission company as a carrier. On the one hand, I will create various types of works beneficial to women's growth and provide a platform for them to create works.

In recent years, with the continuous improvement of women's economic strength, "her economy" and "her consumption" have become important forces in promoting the steady growth of social economy. In terms of market potential, "her economy" has a wide range of radiation, including women's fashion sectors such as beauty, clothing and leisure. From the perspective of consumer strength, women have become one of the main players in online consumption.

I believe that, regardless of the theme of the times or social trend, respecting their subject status, developing "her economy" and safeguarding their rights and interests will remain the trend in the future.

Culture is so sustainable as to unlimitedly transcend time and space. As a contemporary young entrepreneur, I will firmly adhere to the cultural industry for positive energy advocated by the era under the guidance of the core socialist values.

In the future, I will bring together more people to fulfill the duty and mission entrusted by the times. On the one hand, we must adhere to the direction of advanced socialist culture, establish a high degree of cultural consciousness and cultural self-confidence, and help develop children's education and pay attention to women's rights and interests. On the other, we will stride toward the grand goal for Chinese civilization to go global and for building China into a socialist and culturally strong country.

11 Power of Youth

The young generation will surely have much to offer, and make a difference.

As the Chinese youth, what can we do in this new era? Based on this, we have started Asian Civil Media Co., Ltd., are preparing China Colorful Civilization Development Foundation, and will hold "Asian Plan 100" series of activities, hoping to contribute our bit to the community of common destiny for Asia and that of common destiny for mankind.

Cultural Confidence & National Rejuvenation

Behind all actions there is always the support of spiritual and cultural strength. Culture, like an invisible hand, is capable of generating a mighty inspiring power in the process of learning and transforming the world.

While in the new era, when everyone is sounding the bugle for the Chinese Dream, how can a Chinese youth button right his first button of life or take the crucial step in life?

Behind this is the cultivation of core socialist values, the promotion of the advanced socialist culture, the great vision and all-inclusiveness oriented to the future.

Today, the role and status of culture have risen to a new level. Cultural self-confidence and national rejuvenation, strong culture and nationality have become a close and inseparable whole. In the years of this great era, what action should our younger generations take for carrying forward the power of advanced culture?

The river of time flows on, and there is no return of time. Every generation of youth has its own experience. In the context of this era, we are determined to establish a company for the cultural output of positive energy, advocate values of positive energy, and strive to be humanistic inheritors and champions of Asian civilization, and builders of the community of common destiny for Asia and that of common destiny for mankind.

Chinese civilization for thousands of years has become the gene rooted in every Chinese. We will carry forward positive energy and publicize advanced socialist culture with our youthful power as a response to the truth shown by General Secretary Xi Jinping, "Without a high degree of cultural self-confidence and no cultural prosperity, there will be no rejuvenation of the Chinese nation."

Comprehending General Secretary Xi Jinping's Governance of China, we young entrepreneurs will do things as usual. Under the guidance of "Do not forget the original aspiration, absorb what is foreign and be future-oriented," we will assimilate the world culture with the spirit of great breadth of mind. Based on the global vision, our culture with positive energy will be able to go global and let the power of China be felt by the world, and we hope to encourage our counterparts around the world to strive hard, keep high spirits and be all-inclusive. Culture, no matter when, is the existence that transcends all boundaries. Tang Xianzu has been known as William Shakespeare of the East, created their own brilliant pearls in different countries, which has enabled them to shine throughout the world history.

Living in the same period to Shakespeare, Chinese playwright Tang Xianzu, known as "the Oriental Shakespeare", had created world-famous works like *Peony Pavilion, The Purple Hairpin* and others. The heroes in the works above have enriched every aspect of human life with many famous sayings like "Once love starts, it goes deep."

Today, as we look at the diverse cultures of the world on its stage, we must grasp the pulse of the times and listen to its voice. The world culture shines brightly in exchanges and produces a wonderful "chemical reaction" in mutual appreciation. The power and charm of advanced culture belong not only to one country but also to the rest world.

The philosopher Hegel had once marveled at the enduring destiny of China owing to its history and culture. It had also made the historian Arnold J. Toynbe admire the continuity of Chinese civilization.[1] Our cultural self-confidence is rooted in the broad-mindedness and all-inclusiveness of the Chinese nation, and the deep cultural root is the inexhaustible source of our future literary works.

Culture has a long-lasting and deep explosive power. It influences the thought and behavior of an individual, the growth and development of the next generation, and the future direction of a country and the world. How do we view the leading role of advanced culture and how to treat the culture of positive energy from positive thinking?

Self-cultivating, family regulating, country ruling as well as the promotion of a community of common destiny for mankind, all embody the role of culture. The world's multi-polarization, economic globalization, cultural diversity, social informati- zation, and the complicated future all require the power of culture to lead us forward.

---

[1] Wu Xiaoming,"Inspire Cultural Innovation and Creativity with Cultural Self-confidence", *Guangming Daily*, 7 March, 2019.

Asian Civilization & Youthful Mission

The Asian Civilization Dialogue Conference is of great significance.

At this historic node of the exchanges and mutual learning of Asian civilization and the historic moment of the development of human civilization, we intend to start a foundation based on the following three points:

In response to General Secretary Xi Jinping's call for the keynote speech at the opening ceremony of the Asian Civilization Dialogue Conference, we are striving to be the inheritors and champions of Asian civilization, creating a beautiful future for Asian and world civilizations. At the opening ceremony of the Conference, General Secretary Xi Jinping delivered a keynote speech entitled "Deepening Civilizations and Exchanges and Building a Community of Common destiny for Asia" and issued a call to the people of the world to jointly create a better future for Asian and world civilizations.

Therefore, relying on the launch of "Asian Plan 100" series, Asian Civilization & Culture Media Co., Ltd., which focuses on the creation of videos and literary works with positive energy is to be set up for promoting the mutual understanding of Asian people and the exchange and learning of different cultural forms, highlighting the rich and enduring vitality of Asian culture and deeply conforming to the development appeal of the community of common destiny for Asia and that of common destiny for mankind.

Create a series of "Chinese Youth Name Cards" and lead the inheritance of Asian civilization with youthful power. Youth is the future of the nation, the hope of the country, and a powerful force for strengthening exchanges and dialogues of Asian civilization for inheritance.

Therefore, the contemporary Chinese youth need to understand and follow the general trend, be oriented to the future, uphold equality and respect, abandon arrogance and prejudice, deepen the understanding of Chinese civilization and other cultural differences, and promote exchanges and dialogues and harmonious coexistence among different civilizations, be friendly to the neighbors, work together to build a better future, fulfill the youthful responsibility and mission by the times, strive to be the inheritors and champions of Asian civilization, and strive to be a holder of the "China Youth Name Card", thus creating a new Asia in mutual learning and understanding. In the process of inheritance, we will create a new peak of Asian civilization.

The Foundation is a fair, just, transparent and sustainable public welfare platform for the exchange, inheritance and protection of Asian civilization under the guidance of Xi Jinping's socialism with Chinese characteristics for the New Era.

It is the aim with the Foundation to lead the Asian civilization with the youthful power, bring together more young people from Asian countries, promote mutual understanding between people of different countries, deepen exchanges and mutual understanding between different cultural forms, and to create a community of common destiny for Asia and that of common destiny for mankind.

Asian civilization in history, which created the glory of mankind and originated thousands of years Before Christ, birthed a rich human civilization from the valleys of the Tigris-Euptuate, the Indus-Ganga, and the Yellow River-Yangtze River. Under the view of Great Harmony, various civilizations have merged. The ancient commercial roads such as the Silk Road, the Tea Road, and the Spice Road and today's "One Belt, One Road", "Two Corridors and One Circle" and "Eurasian

Economic Union" have all broadened the channels of civilization exchanges and mutual learning, and the whole of Asia has developed and grown strong owing to the promotion of civilization and culture.

A look in history will trace back to the social ideal of "Universal Harmony" proposed by Confucius thousands of years ago, which stressed on "harmony". At the beginning of the 20th century, the ideal of "Great Harmony of the World" proposed by Dr. Sun Yat-sen was also "harmony". In his "Three Principles of the People", there was no gap between the rich and the poor in the future society, or injustice by a few rich oppressing the poor. In his concept, he fully realized the bourgeois concept equality of the "of the people, by the people and for the people", which truly embodies the "Universal Harmony" advocated by the ancients.

Back to the present, under the background of the times, the Foundation is an echo of the historical mission and the responsibility for a young Chinese. We will focus on promoting the core issues of Asian civilization exchanges and mutual understanding, strive for the successful completion of Asian civilization exchanges and mutual understanding of domestic issues, adhere to the direction of international development with global thinking and strategies, and integrate resources on a larger scale. A higher level of promotion and mutual understanding of Asian civilization.

Asian Plan 100

Facing the common challenges of the world and moving towards a better life in the future, we need not only the power of economic science and technology, but also that of cultural civilization. At this moment, the convening of the Asian Civilization Dialogue Conference has provided a new platform for promoting equal dialogues, mutual exchanges and mutual enlightenment among civilizations in Asia and the world.

One in a new era should shoulder his responsibility. Therefore, I and young writer Liao Yujing responded to the call of the times and planned to draw up the "Asian Plan 100." This is a non-profit society aiming to establish a fair, just, transparent and sustainable development for the exchange, inheritance and protection of Asian Civilization, based on China Colorful Civilization Development Foundation, and it follows the guidance of Xi Jinping Thought on Socialism with Chinese Characteristics for the New Era. In the future, the Foundation will have its branches to assist foreign affairs, pubilicity, education, culture and other departments concerned in conducting various activities.

First, support and fund 100 high-end forums on Asian civilization exchanges in China; support and fund 100 Asian civilization exchange activities organized by Chinese social organizations.

Civilizations communicate because of diversity, mutual learning through exchanges, and develop and prosper through mutual learning. As an important birthplace of human civilization, Asia has created brilliant achievements. The 100 civilized communication forums and activities are in response to General Secretary Xi Jinping's appeal at the Asian Civilization Dialogue Conference. They insist on exchanges and mutual learning with other civilizations and jointly write a brilliant new chapter for Asian civilization.

Secondly, it supports and funds 100 activities to be held in China for selecting outstanding figures of Asian Civilization; supports, funds and rewards 100 outstanding contributors to the exchanges of Asian civilization; supports and funds the selection of 100 holders of "Chinese Youth Name Card" for promoting Asian civilization exchanges.

People are always the core of the development of the times. Talented people promote the development of science and technology and create miracles in the world. Publicizing outstanding figures and selecting outstanding talent and contributors can not only spread the positive energy, but also let the general public understand the people who inherit the national spirit and contribute to the country and so on. It can also help establish a correct world outlook, outlook on life and values in the whole society.

"China Youth Name Card", which promotes the progress of Asian civilization, intends to touch Asia and even the world with the images of Chinese youth, which is not only a means of publicity for Chinese youth and Chinese culture, but also a way of telling Chinese stories from a global perspective, showing the socialist achievements of spiritual civilization with Chinese characteristics and reflecting the cultural confidence of the Chinese people.

"Asian Plan 100" will also support and fund 100 series of activities for promoting the exchange of Asian civilization outside China. Let the world understand

Asia, let civilizations exchange and learn from each other, and build a community of common destiny for Asia and that of common destiny for mankind.

"Asian Plan 100" series of activities is a powerful manifestation of the young generation following the times and its responsibility. On the one hand, it closely matches the development background shared by the countries in the world, its main voice of exchange and integration, and the realistic needs through the exchange and mutual understanding of Asian civilization in the new era. On the other, based on China with the world in mind, we seek exchanges and dialogues between different civilizations in Asia and the world, harmonious coexistence, and exchanges between different cultures with a thick international color.

"Asia 100 Program" series of activities is a concrete manifestation of the exchanges between different civilizations, nationalities, countries and regions in the world.

Diverse and colorful civilizations have built a rich and colorful world civilization. Asian countries, separated by mountains and rivers, have common ground and differences in civilization. No single civilization can be judged superior to another or can one replace the other. General Secretary Xi Jinping's initiative to hold the Asian Civilization Dialogue Conference has established an important platform for the exchange of different civilizations between Asian countries. In the current situation, it can be said that it is timely and significant.

Asian countries share the same fate. "Asian Plan 100" is based on this with the hope that the dialogue and blending of Asian civilizations will be strengthened, mutual understanding will be enhanced, and Asia will create and share common prosperity.

As the young generation, we will uphold the values of open and inclusive Asian civilization, strengthen exchanges and mutual learning with other civilizations, work with the young people from other countries, jointly open a new situation for the progress of Asian civilization, and contribute to building the community of common destiny for Asia and that of common destiny for mankind and to building a harmonious world as well.

12 Chinese civilization & World Civilization

Chinese culture is profound and profound and has a long history. For a long time, Chinese civilization has been the core of Asian civilization and even world civilization.

Today, as the destiny of mankind is united, the power of culture cannot be underestimated. As the youth in China, Asia and even the world, we must move from China to Asia and then to the world and continue to speak for Chinese civilization and world civilization.

Chinese Nation & Great Harmony

The "Great Harmony of the World" is the ideal social blueprint pursued by the ancestors of the past dynasties. It also contains the Chinese people's deep concern for the common destiny of the surrounding world and the people. The phrase of "Great Harmony" first appeared in the *Book of Rites* • *Liyun*, which described an ideal social state of "all for one, one for all."

In the society of great harmony, the sage and talent are valued, and everyone is honest and live in harmony. People not only support their parents, educate their children, but also let all the elderly enjoy their declining years and all young ones grow up healthily. Everyone has a good home, and no one is greedy for money or after personal gain. Western Han ritualist Dai Sheng believed that "universal harmony is a just cause to be pursued for the common good."

Seen from this, there is something in common between China's earliest great harmony and Communism of a thousand years later. In the subsequent long history, the combination of the thought of "Great Harmony of the World" and the times has formed a unique view of its own while containing more Chinese breadth of mind.

He Xiu, of the Eastern Han Dynasty and master of Gongyang School, once proposed history evolved "from the troubled world, to the trouble-free world and to the peaceful world", and the last of which is quite similar to the society of great harmony.

At the turn of the Ming and Qing Dynasties, Huang Zongxi proposed that "the chaos or peace of the world concerns not the rise or fall of a royal family, but the sorrow or joy of the public", believing that Xia, Shang and Zhou Dynasties were the golden age of human society, and intending for the "equality for all" system to be established after that.

In the late Qing Dynasty, with the intervention of Western forces, China staggered into modern times. While in such internal and external strife, the Chinese longing for a universally harmonious society bore a strong patriotism.

Kang Youwei said in his *Book of Great Harmony*, "Born in a troubled world, I have witnessed what suffering is like, and have been thinking in private of a way out, only to find that universal peace and harmony will do." He advocated doing away with the "nine worlds" and transforming "Great Harmony in China" into "Great Harmony in the world".

In order to strive for a favorable international environment shortly after the founding of New China, the Chinese delegation to the Bandung Conference in Indonesia. In response to the attacks on socialism by some countries, China pointed out that, "According to the principle of mutual respect for sovereignty and territorial integrity, mutual non-aggression, non-interference in each other's internal affairs, equality and mutual benefit, countries with different social systems can achieve peace. The discord and estrangement that colonial rule has caused between Asian and African countries should not continue. We should respect each other and eliminate the doubts and fears that may exist between us. The Chinese delegation is here seeking unity rather than quarreling."

After Chinese Delegation proposed the principle of "seeking common ground while reserving differences", all countries present abandoned their previous suspicions and unanimously discussed and adopted the final bulletin of the Asian-African Conference, including economic cooperation, cultural cooperation, human rights and self-determination, issues of people in the dependent areas, and declaration for promoting world peace and cooperation.

It can be said that the Bandung Conference for dealing with the relationship between countries has become a classic demonstration, at which diplomatic thinking of "harmony without uniformity and coexistence" is of paramount importance.

From ancient times to the present, the spiritual culture of the Chinese nation has always retained the everlasting color of great harmony. General Secretary Xi Jinping repeatedly mentioned the concept of "when the Great Way prevails, a public spirit rules all under Heaven", and quoted Mencius's words, "getting the righteous name and following the best road" for explaining the pursuit of the Chinese nation since ancient times.

The concept of great harmony by the Chinese nation has a long history and a profound influence, which constantly gives off infinite vitality and charm. Now, this concept is taking shape of broad mind, concern for the world, and patriotism.

Universal harmony and peaceful cooperation are both the concepts upheld for thousands of years in Chinese civilization. This philosophy is the "Universal Harmony" that we have been discussing.

When globalization challenges the ideological cultures and values of all countries and nations, should one choose to hear only one voice or promote mutual integration, seek the common ground while reserving the difference, mutual appreciation among various cultures and civilizations? Should one choose to rudely resort to military, economic, and even cultural hegemony for solution or promote equal treatment, peaceful coexistence, and common development among countries and nations?

From the ancient wisdom concerning "Great Harmony", we can find many answers. As far as China is concerned, its essence of the traditional thinking has been integrated into its principle of handling state-to-state relations and active participation in globalization. In today's era of globalization, we are no longer separate individuals or independent of each other because of nationalities. In the new era, "Great Harmony" is not just moral uplift of one's own but some breadth of mind for the rest world. Just as happiness should not be the enjoyment of an independent unit but the shared feeling around the world.

As far as the world is concerned, despite its differences in connotation, this Chinese traditional concept still has some positive reference for promoting the healthy development of globalization in today's world.

The stone tablet in front of the UNESCO Headquarters carries a message, "Since wars begin in the minds of men, it is in the minds of men that the defenses of peace must be constructed." Exchanges and dialogues are always the best way to eliminate the thought of wars and bridge the cultural differences between countries and nations.

In the context of this era, I have initiated China Colorful Civilization Development Foundation to promote cultural exchanges in the Asian region, promote cultural harmony, development and progress, and thus establish a society of "Great Harmony" in Asia. I believe that, on the basis of active exchanges and dialogues, China Colorful Civilization Development Foundation can do some promotion and contribution to the universal harmony in the world.

Community of Common destiny for Mankind

Some people compare the earth to a big ship and the 190-plus countries to its passengers. How can we enable it to sail more smoothly? Only when all the passengers respect each other, cooperate sincerely, and cherish tolerance and exchanges can the ship of "Earth" sail far through the wind and waves, carrying the community of common destiny for all mankind.

We are no stranger to the concept of the community above. More than two thousand years ago, the Greek philosopher Aristotle said, "Human beings are born social animals." Because of this social attribute of theirs, various groups, that is, communities, have gradually been formed for survival and development. As early as in ancient China, the prevailing concept of Huangdi and Laozi had already owned the concept of "community". In the long process of development, traditional cultural concepts such as "harmony of Nature and man" and "harmony without uniformity" have gradually become the cultural genes of today's community of common destiny for mankind.

Human thoughts and steps progress together. At the beginning of the 15th century, Zheng He, a famous Chinese navigator, sailed abroad. The concept of "community" began to be practiced between the ocean and the land.

Despite its largest fleet at the time, none of Zheng He's seven grand voyages was meant for encroachment, but for exchanges of cultures, gifts, and trade. He conveyed the expectation of universal peace of the world.Even now, his Treasure Ship is still regarded as a symbol of "peace", "exchange" or "friendship". In the Singapore Maritime Museum, there is a life-size copy of Zheng He's Treasure Ship.

When time came to the 18th century, the concept of "community" was still there between countries. The United States, which had just gained independence, opened the road of trade and was eager to communicate with the outside world. A US merchant ship named "The Empress of China" sailed from the other side of the Pacific Ocean and completed its first trip to China and the United States. Chinese goods such as porcelain and silk could be seen everywhere on that fully loaded ship. George Washington, first US president, when he heard this, purchased more than 300 pieces of porcelain. To this day, these antiques are still in his former residence and Pennsylvania Museum.

Now, the vast world inhabited by humans has become a small "global village". The distance between people is infinitely narrowed, the relationship between countries is infinitely close, and the concept of community transcends the restriction of time and space.

What is the community of common destiny? Humankind has only one earth, where all nations coexist in one world. In 2012, the 18th CPC National Congress clearly stated that "we must advocate the awareness of a common destiny for mankind and consider the legitimate concern for other countries while pursuing their own interests."

Mencius said in his Tengwengong, "Live in the most spacious house, stay in the most central place and take the broadest road of the world. When accomplished, go with the people, or do it alone." This shows Mencius's thought about what a true man should cher- ish for the community of common destiny for mankind.

Everything can exist in harmony without harming each other, and roads can go in parallel without contradicting each other. When we stand at the height of world history to re-examine the development trend of today's world, the path of peaceful development, an independent foreign policy, and the strategy of mutual benefit and openness is still what we must adhere to in building the community of common destiny for mankind with the people of all countries.

There are two powerful forces in this world, one being armed force and the other is thought. In the long run, the latter is far stronger than the former. To assist the community of common destiny for mankind and move better forward, we must first pay heed to the power of civilized culture.

Liang Qichao once said, "Culture is the valuable common industry accumulated from the human heart." Among the five connotations of the community, the "cultural community" is the foundation for building everything else and an important force for propelling the progress of human civilization and the peaceful development of the world.

To build a community of common destiny for mankind in culture, we must respect the diversity of world civilization. A variety of civilizations is just like the inherent features in each of us. In the long history, mankind has created a colorful civilization. All countries and regions form a map of the world civilization. We cannot deny but should respect individual differences. “Harmony without uniformity” is the ancient wisdom of Chinese civilization, reflecting the human feelings of openness and great breath of mind.

Civilization is the link connecting humanity to exchanges and dialogues. Building a community of common destiny for close neighbors requires the power of civilization. To promote civilized exchanges and mutual learning, and build a cultural community, we must uphold the correct understanding and attitude.

In 2008, at the opening ceremony of the Beijing Olympic Games, various forms of the Chinese character “he” (meaning harmony in English –translator) conveyed to the world Chinese cultural concept of “harmony topping all else”.

Over the Tiananmen Rostrum, the slogan of “Long Live the Great Unity of the World People” is very eye-catching. Today, the community of common destiny for mankind, such a profound practice of it, is a continuation of the ancient Chinese thought of “all countries being one family in harmony and peace.”

So rich and colorful is the world when all kinds of civilizations add beauty and radiance to each other! Every country and nation have contributed to the development of human civilization, which shows why the sea is vast owing to its tolerance of hundreds of rivers. Only by interacting with and promoting each other can the development of world civilization be full of vitality.

What every civilization continues is the blood of the country and nation. Undoubtedly, the community of common destiny for mankind must be preceded by that of common destiny for close neighbors. China's long national border and complex geopolitical environment, which means quite a challenge for creating such a community. But we are connected with the surrounding mountains and rivers, and building it is the general trend.

The ancient trade route had once helped bears exchanges and dialogues between civi- lizations and witnessed such events of exchange of the Asian people. As an important part of world civilization, the brilliant Asian civilization is the common spiritual wealth of mankind. Building a community of common destiny for mankind has a long way to go and requires the hard struggle of young people from generation to generation. As Chinese and Asian youth, at this historic node of the Asian civilization exchanges for mutual understanding, we are preparing to start China Colorful Civilization Development Foundation as inheritors and champions of Asian civilization and with the intent of creating a bright future for Asian and world civilizations.

Building a community of common destiny for mankind is a beautiful vision of all living on earth, who can hardly leave each other as their connection is getting closer and closer. If this world, like a big ship, intends to sail far through winds and waves, requires the concerted efforts of all countries. And What China is working hard for is nothing but the vision to be achieved through the great unity of the people of the world.

The World as We Expect

More than 1,300 years ago, a monk set out from the Capital city of Chang'an for his long journey to the west. After untold hardships, he finally arrived in India and got the true Scripture while spreading making Chinese civilization known to the other Asian countries all the way.This monk was Xuan Zang. In his later book *Records on the Western Regions of the Great Tang Empire*, he recorded thus, "I have traveled through one hundred and ten kingdoms, and heard of twenty eight; I have read about some of them in some books, and the names of the rest I have learnt about now."

The Tang Dynasty, as a period of active foreign exchanges in history, had contacts with some countries in Asia, Africa, and even Europe. Xuan Zang's west-bound trip is a microcosm of the Dynasty's interaction with the rest world. Other examples include Jianzhen's travel to Japan and Abenonakamaro's travel to China. This is a romantic dynasty with magnificent and colorful colors. Some historians have commented that "the Tang Dynasty had a cosmopolitan temperament," as it had a fairly high international prestige. Today, Communities inhabited by Chinese around the world still bear the name of "Chinatown".

During the Tang Dynasty, under the strong influence of Chinese culture, North Korea, Japan, Vietnam and other countries came to China to study. Gathered around the central civilization of China, the Asian countries at that time lived in great harmony.

More than 1,300 years later, General Secretary Xi Jinping, while attending the Asian Civilization Dialogue Conference, remarked that people are the best carrier for civilized exchanges and mutual understanding. Deepening the people-to-people exchanges is an important way to eliminate barriers and misunderstandings and promote their mutual understanding.[1] True as General Secretary Xi Jinping says, people in this vast environment of the world are the carrier and transmitter of civilization. Today's world is undergoing rapid changes, and the exchanges and collisions of culture and civilization are of daily occurrence. Therefore, we hold a higher expectation of the world and its civilization.

Peace is the foundation of development. With a peaceful internal and external environment, all countries can develop their economy with a peaceful mind, improve their livelihood and thrive their cultural and scientific undertakings. Only with a vast peaceful environment can the world usher in development, without which few nations can remain peaceful. As the historical law has shown, only by keeping a global vision, adhering to the path of peaceful development, and continuously expanding mutually beneficial cooperation with other countries, can we better achieve self-development, better cope with global challenges, and contribute to its development. Therefore, all countries in the world must respect each other and live in harmony, let civilized exchanges cross national borders and go beyond time and space, and "maintain a peaceful time that is more precious than gold."

Economy is the material guarantee and strong support for the development and progress of culture and politics. A no small number of people across the world are now still in poverty. In this regard, all the countries there must work together to promote a more inclusive, balanced and win-win economic globalization, jointly eliminate poverty and backwardness, create a life of carefree life for future gener-

---

[1] "Xi Jinping Attended the Opening Ceremony of the Asian Civilization Dialogue and Delivered a Keynote Speech ", *People's Daily*, 16 May, 2019.

ations, and let thousands of households see what real happiness is.

Deng Chao, an associate researcher with the Institute of World History at the Institute of Chinese History, said, "People have found that such characteristics of Asian civilization as benevolence, moderation and tolerance have a corrective effect on Western civilization. General Secretary Xi Jinping proposed to build a community of common destiny for Asia, which both reflects on the world his strong concern for and pursuit of peace, and expresses China's hope for building peace, prosperity and development in Asia."

Culture, "so smooth and silent", has a powerful power. To achieve sustainable development, all countries and nations in the world must strengthen cultural exchanges and mutual understanding and consolidate the community of common destiny for mankind.

In the future, with the rise of all countries in the world, different civilizations will play an increasingly important role in bridging national disputes, promoting world peace and development, and strengthening mutual trust and mutual trust among the nations.

In recent decades, many countries in Asia have opened their doors and actively integrated into the historical trend of globalization, got on the fast-growing international express train. In the future, all countries in the world will open their doors even wider.

In the future, we expect to see various nations in Asia respect mutual differences, talk with each other on an equal footing, appreciate each other and continue to promote the innovation and progress of civilization and make new contributions to the world civilization under the principle of all-inclusiveness.

Chinese Youth as the World Expects

On the journey of China's ups and downs in the past century, the struggle of its young people's enthusiasm has been engraved in history. Their mission of the times, youthful dream, and determination to struggle have always been shining in the long history, inspiring all the Chinese youth from generation to generation.

China today is different from what it was. At present, it is the developing country with the strongest overall national strength in the world. With its constant rise in international status, China is undergoing profound and extensive changes. Our contemporary youth are at an extremely fast and active moment in China, with unprecedented opportunities and challenges.

In 1979, when the world knew very little about China owing to its very few contacts with it. At that time, there were only a handful of Chinese who could be seen in Sweden. However, in its few decades of reform and opening up, China has changed its image from separation to integration, so its people can be seen all over the world.

At present, China's relations with the world have already undergone a historic change, and its future and destiny increasingly connected to the rest of the world. The world needs China more and more. Professor Danny Quay of the London School of Economics and Political Science said, "After 10 or 20 years, the global economic center will fall between China and India." So, while assisting the world peace, prosperity and development and building a community of shared human destiny, the Chinese youth facing both opportunities and challenges of the new era will have to shoulder their mission and responsibility.

What kind of Chinese youth does the world look forward to? Here is the answer.

Having a global vision by standing on the height of the world to accommodate multiculturalism is a sense that Chinese youth should cultivate.

In the past few decades, China has been rapidly developing from a poor and backward country to a major one in economy and trade. At the same time with its rapid advancement of international status and comprehensive national strength, China's right to speak has also increased. At a time when the world is closely integrated, the Chinese youth are playing an increasingly important role in the international community.

China's development cannot be separated from the world, and vice versa. As young people of the new era, we must strengthen exchanges and contacts with the world and build friendship with the people of all countries with an open and inclusive mind. At the same time, we must show the outstanding look of the Chinese youth and perform well our role as a bridge in letting the world and China understand each other.

Lu Xun once said that the young people "have so much energy that they can level whatever deep forest, plant trees where the wilderness lies and dig wells when they meet the desert." Young people, filled with vigor and vitality, are the hope of the world and will surely take over the baton of the future.

Youth is the hope of the country and the nation, and it represents the future of the world. The Chinese youth are to go global but must first of all firmly believe in their love of the motherland.

The Chinese youth to go global won't get any respect if they don't love their country in the first place. A person who denies his own nationality and feels no gratefulness to his country, won't be recognized however talented he is, either.

In the face of a beautiful era and a better life, we must think with great indebtedness where it is from like one who drinks water. We were born in socialist China and enjoy the peaceful environment and opportunities of the times created by the country. Once we be- come talented, it is a reasonable choice to repay the society and be grateful to the country. While cultivating our vision of the world, none of us young people must forget our root. When learning about the world's diverse cultures and values, we must understand how to maintain our own mainstream values, seek common ground while reserving differences, and stick to harmony without uniformity.

As the backbone of the times, we Chinese youth must distinguish between right and wrong and stand firm in the face of a complex world change.

To let China and the world understand each other is the mission for our contemporary youth. The world is rich and diverse, and the future is vast. One won't know how big the world is unless he goes out into it. Once outside China, they represent the image of the country. They must be able to tell good China stories, showcase their role, and actively promote foreign exchanges.

The world is fast changing and the knowledge and information are being updated from day to day. Time waits for no man, so we young people must seize every opportunity, keep pace with the times, follow its trend, and constantly enrich ourselves.

Constantly learn the world's excellent culture, technology, etc., broaden the horizons of vision, accelerate the renewal of knowledge, and optimize the structure of knowledge systems. Live and learn.

As the contemporary youth, we are most energetic and vigorous, and have the most impetus and motivation. We must continue to study all the time, be models for other youth, talented youth, and contribute our youthful power to the world.

The Chinese youth must always be innovative and support the world with a steady stream of vitality. Innovation is an important driving force for the development and a key strategy for the future. Innovation is the driving force for thriving the country and the progress and prosperity of the world.

The contemporary youth should stand in the forefront of innovation, dare to think, to do and to be the first, actively participate in innovative practices, and make their own achievements. The world expects to own talented people with an innovative spirit, and mankind needs innovation to drive its development. In the vast international arena, what innovative people will bring about is the power to change the world.

The contemporary Chinese youth must be brave to take responsibility for the times and have lofty ideals and ambitions. The future of the country and of the world is to be placed on the youth, so General Secretary Xi Jinping encourages them to try to be "saintly and talented people," to be involved in the world of the new era, so as to let their ideals take root in reality and make their struggle the most beautiful youthful color.

Postscript
Positive Energy & New Vision of Civilization

While I am writing this book, guests from 47 countries and five continents are all in Beijing for the Asian Civilization Dialogue Conference.

This makes me feel so proud and excited. Nowadays, the uncertainty and instability of the international situation is getting more prominent and all the consensus hinges on exchanges and contacts. This Conference has offered a new opportunity for the promotion of equal dialogues and exchanges between the civilizations of Asia and the world so as to enlighten and inspire each other.

As one of the Chinese young entrepreneurs, I've been closely following the country's progress, for I know that every achievement by entrepreneurs is closely related to the journey of my country.

Successful entrepreneurs previous to us share a common conclusion that those who have made it are all followers of the times. As I understand, if an entrepreneur is to achieve sustained success, he must be good at grasping and transmitting the kindling spark of civilization, and actively participate in the cause for advancing human civilization, so as to truly keep his long-term success.

As described in *Modern Journey* many years ago, a worthless grain of sand can be turned into magical glass, telescopes, microscopes and flasks through the hands of craftsmen, who have brought along science, which brought modernity.

Many years later, even the most slow-witted people knew how to make glass, but the present generation of craftsmen have turned sand into silicon and fiber for transmitting all human wisdom and civilization to every promised place around the world. A great postmodern era is now coming.

In fact, whether in this great postmodern or its early stage, the advancement of human civilization is the true theme and core logic. The construction of a community of common destiny for mankind based on civilization will surpass any period in history today.

A look back at the history and into the world shows that civilizations communicate because of diversity, mutual learning through exchanges, and development through mutual learning. From the ancient commercial roads such as the Silk Road to the present, "One Belt and One Road", the world civilizations have promoted each other and developed by means of exchanges and mutual learning.

As a young entrepreneur in China, I will try to run my enterprise well, and better pass on new commercial civilization and positive energy; I must cherish the root of Chinese civilization and enable to it bloom in the world civilization.

This book is but some ideas, insight and understanding based on my own experience, positive energy and new commercial civilization.

I have always been thinking that the positive energy of human nature and the rational power of civilization are the two tracks that constitute the way we march forward on. Therefore, no matter how busy I may be every day, I seldom stop thinking about how to pass the fire of positive energy and civilization. I wish that this work of mine and other efforts might help illuminate the way forward for some youngsters and sincerely hope that more people can join me and work together to create a better future for world civilization!

Here, when this book is approaching its end, the mission for the young Asians and even those of the world has just begun. I remember a friend who said that in a forum for international youth exchanges, no matter which country they come from, everyone says " I have been to Afghanistan, I have seen...", "I found when I was in South Africa...", "In the two months of my presence in Pakistan...", there are not a few Chinese among them, and everyone is committed to solving Asian and world problems together. These are also the main reasons why I firmly intend this book for Asian youth and help establish the China Colorful Civilization Development Foundation.

The completion of this book is inseparable from the support and help of many people, of whom I'd like most to thank my good friend Liao Yujing, an excellent young writer. In 2012, he was named by the British *Financial Times* as "One of the most promising post-80s writers in China"; in 2015, he won the 7th New Artistic Figures Award; in 2018, he was selected for China Influential Positive Energy Writers Award. The theme, direction, and viewpoint of this book partake of his wisdom and hard work.

I'd like to thank Dr. Zhu Wei, Dr. Shi Lichun, Dr. Sun Honglin and others of Southwest Jiaotong University for their constructive suggestions and unique perspectives.

In addition, I owe my thanks to Koalacan, a team full of vigor and dreams for their deep involvement in content creation and book operation in the past 5 years. This team has more than 10 years of content planning and operation experience. Unlike others, Koalacan has been commissioned to this with a great sense of mission and made its own contributions to documenting this era. We'd like to thank Prof. Cao Shunfa for his good English rendering of this very book.

Finally, I'd like to thank all the readers for their patience, for this book would be of little value without their reading. I hope that it can convey to all the youth the value of hard struggle for the country and the nation, contribute my share to the two Centenary Goals and Chinese Dream.

Wen Zeping at Lanjiao Media
on the evening of August 26, 2019